Exhibition

1825 1975

Shildon August 24th to 30th 1975.
Locomotives and Rolling Stock.
Opening Times: 11.00 to 1900 hours.
Prices: Sunday, Monday, Saturday Adult £1. Child 50p.
Tuesday, Wednesday, Thursday, Friday Adult 60p. Child 30p. O.A.P. 30p.

Grand Steam Cavalcade

Sunday August 31st, 1975.
Route: Stockton & Darlington Railway from Shildon to Heighington.
Starting Time: 14.00 hrs.
Grandstands: £3.00. Enclosures: Adult 50p, Child 25p.
Cheques payable to: Steam 150.
All advance bookings to: Visit Northumbria, 7 North Road, Durham City. Tel. 0325/65042.

Admission to all exhibitions is subject to the specific condition that the Exhibitors, Joint Committee, British Rail, their employees, servants and agents accept no liability for injury or death to persons entering, or for loss or damage to their property, no matter howsoever caused and irrespective of any negligence by British Rail, the Joint Committee, their employees, servants or agents.

All information in this guide is believed to be correct at the time of going to press. However, with such a large event many details have not been finalised and the Organisers reserve the right to alter and amend both exhibits and the programme without prior notification should this become necessary.

EXHIBITION ADMINISTRATION

North Road Station, Darlington, Co. Durham. Tel. 0325/54150.

Joint Committee for Stockton & Darlington Railway 150 Celebrations

---

President: Lord Downe
Chairman: Councillor J. Tatchell

LOCAL AUTHORITIES

Durham County Council
Cleveland County Council
Darlington Borough Council
Sedgefield District Council
Stockton Borough Council
Wear Valley District Council
The Former:
Bishop Auckland U.D.C.
Darlington C.B.C.
Shildon U.D.C.
Teeside C.B.C.

ASSOCIATED ORGANISATIONS

British Rail
British Rail Engineering
National Coal Board
Association of Railway Preservation Societies
Northumbrian Tourist Board
Yorkshire Tourist Board
North of England Newspapers
Middlesborough Evening Gazette
B.B.C. Radio Cleveland
Northern Arts
Stephenson Locomotive Society
Railway Correspondence & Travel Society
North Eastern Railway Association
North Eastern Locomotive Preservation Group
North Yorkshire Moors Railway
Steam Power Trust 65
Railway & Canal Historical Society
North East Industrial Archaelogical Council
North of England Open Air Museum

LOCAL CELEBRATION COMMITTEES

Darlington
Shildon
Stockton

President's Welcome

The Rt. Hon. Viscount Downe

"That it may be lawful after the passing of this Act to make loco-motive or mobile engines and to use and employ the same upon the said railway."

A new railway needed the authority of Parliament and these words were proposed as part of the Stockton and Darlington Railway Act 1823. They caused some surprise to Lord Shaftesbury's secretary, who thinking that a "loco-motive" must be some strange unheard of animal, struck it from the draft wording. It needed careful explanation from the M.P. for Northumberland to legitimise the strange beast for inclusion in the Act.

Men of the North East of England had joined together to promote an idea so novel that it was introducing new words to the language, and as the day approached to open it, local excitement mounted. Up to 50,000 people watched the opening train pulled by a "loco-motive" numbered "1" which set off from Shildon East Lane.

Now 150 years later we can see with the perspective of history the results which followed that train from Shildon. Distances shrank, travel became generally practical, and choice of product spread in shop and factory. In this commemorative exhibition we can all see examples of the machinery and methods which made these changes possible.

Building the Stockton & Darlington Railway needed the skills and efforts of many hundreds of men, and I wonder if staging the Rail 150 Exhibition has involved fewer. We owe deep debts of gratitude. Durham and Cleveland County Councils have provided financial help, facilities and people. The exhibits are owned by individuals, societies, British Rail, the National Railway Museum, and these have not only been generously lent (sometimes at considerable inconvenience to their owners) but brought to a high

Tindale

state of preparation. British Rail Engineering has been a constant ally, and Flying Scotsman Enterprises have stage managed the movement of locomotives and rolling stock, generously fuelled by the National Coal Board. We are most fortunate that Mr. William Whitelaw has agreed to open this exhibition—and we greet him as a neighbour and grandson of a Chairman of the L.N.E.R. There are men and women throughout this region, and beyond, who have put in long hours doing the countless jobs without which there could be no exhibition. They are the true descendants of the founders of the Stockton and Darlington, from an area which in 1825 built a railway, and in 1975 build oil rigs, nuclear power plant, chemicals and electronics.

In this exhibition we offer a warm welcome to our visitors, and look back at the past with pride—and forward to the future with confidence.

RAIL 150 EXHIBITION OPENING MONDAY 25th AUGUST, 1975

Rt. Hon. William Whitelaw C.H., M.C., M.P.

As part of the opening ceremony the name *George Stephenson* is to be conferred on the L.M.S. Class 5MT locomotive No. 4767.

When the delegates to the International Railway Conference of 1925 arrived at the Faverdale Exhibition they were received by the Chairman of the L.N.E.R., Mr. William Whitelaw.

Our distinguished visitor today, William Stephen Ian Whitelaw, is his grandson, who after going to Winchester and then Cambridge, fought with distinction in the Royal Scots Guards during the Second World War.

He chose politics as his career and now represents the constituency of Penrith & the Borders. Several important positions have been entrusted to him by Conservative governments. However he is best known for his handling of the delicate situation in Northern Ireland. Since then he has been Chairman of the Conservative Party and is now Deputy Leader of the opposition.

L.N.E.R. No. 2563 William Whitelaw 1925 Procession Photomatic

Locomotion Trust

Note from the Editor

ALAN BOWMAN

It was the skill and energy of men such as George Stephenson and Timothy Hackworth which designed the locomotives and built the railways. Men like Pease and Backhouse took these achievements and exploited them to the advantage of industry and trade. The genius and greatness of these men and their successors was celebrated in 1875, again in 1925 and now in 1975 an exciting programme of events has been arranged in the North East.

We are proud of our engineers whose work excels in such projects as the design of bridges, equipment for the chemical industry, the development of nuclear power, fine ships and oil rigs. As we celebrate the 150th anniversary of railways let us also remember that our engineers are building a new steel complex at Lackenby and are piping ashore the first supplies of North Sea oil at Teesmouth—the start of a new era.

The **Rail 150 Exhibition** of Locomotives, Rolling Stock, and other relics is on a scale unlikely to be repeated. The Grand Steam Cavalcade is expected to include over thirty steam locomotives, including a replica of Locomotion No. 1. The Cavalcade will run for a distance of four miles and will take about two hours to pass.

In this souvenir guide we hope by directing your attention to the merit and significance of the exhibits to enhance the understanding and enjoyment of these celebrations. Limitation of space prevents a full description of all the exhibits but there will be opportunities to meet the exhibitors and to appreciate their enthusiasm and pride in achievement.

At the time of writing, arrangements for the exhibition are not yet completed. Such details as the lay-out of the Exhibition, and the order of Cavalcade will be published on a News-sheet, available free at the Exhibition on presentation of this Guide Book.

Railways and Steam Locomotives still have a fascination for all the family and we are sure that your visits to the Rail 150 Exhibitions, Museums, and other Railway Events in the North East will make 1975 a memorable year.

A. M. BOWMAN
April, 1975.

Post Script

The preparation of this souvenir guide book, whilst the details of the exhibition & cavalcade are being finalised, has caused many problems. As editor I must express by appreciation to the contributors and particularly to the editorial team without whose help this book would not have gone to press on time.

Photo Precision Ltd. of St. Ives, Huntingdon who have undertaken the design work and printing. The pleasant helpfulness of their executives and skill of their staff have made my task very much easier.

A.B.
May, 1975.

Opening of the Stockton & Darlington Railway
Displayed in Darlington Museum

Dobbin
Reproduced by courtesy of Darlington Borough Council

ICI

Stockton & Darlington Railway— Its Place in History

by P .W. B. Semmens, M.A., F.R.I.C., M.B.C.S. Chairman of the Stephenson Locomotive Society.

For the present generation, it is difficult to realise what life was like before the coming of the railways made it possible to move people and goods easily around the country. In the course of our business life nowadays, many of us make the 500-mile journey to London and back by train in the course of a single day, eating and working as we travel. However, for our predecessors before the coming of the railways, one hundred and fifty years ago, looking southwards from the high ground at Sedgefield, the line of the Cleveland Hills, only a few miles to the south, would have effectively represented the geographic limit of the world most of them hoped to see during their lifetime.

Without the millions of tons of freight that are carried every year by the railways, we would not be able to enjoy the standard of living we now take for granted. Today the average motorist uses something like a ton of petrol each year in his car driving around the countryside on business or pleasure. It is the railways' bulk inland distribution system which they operate for the oil companies that makes this fuel available for those of us who fill up away from the refineries around our coast. Not only are our minerals, fuels and goods brought to us by rail, but in many places our town wastes are transported away by them as well. It is thus very appropriate that we should, from time to time, look back on the events of the past and take stock of the railways' contributions to our prosperity.

This year's railway events in the North-East are the most extensive since the celebrations for the Centenary of the Stockton & Darlington Railway in 1925, which are still talked about by those who were fortunate to see or take part in them. As a result of all this publicity for the Stockton & Darlington Railway, there may be many people who believe that this was the first railway or that *Locomotion* was the first steam railway locomotive. In fact, when the first Act of Parliament for the construction of the Stockton & Darlington Railway received the Royal Assent in 1821, it was the twenty-first Railway Bill to be passed since the beginning of the century. Nevertheless in its conception, the Stockton & Darlington Railway was a far more ambitious project than any of those schemes that had preceded it. The main line was planned to cover just over 26 miles from the collieries in the Witton Park area and pass via Darlington to the port of Stockton on the River Tees.

It was a public railway in the same sense as a road is referred to as a public highway: anyone paying the appropriate charges and observing the necessary operating rules could carry his own goods over the line in his own vehicles. It was thus following the pattern set by the Surrey Iron Railway, the first public railway, which had been opened in 1803, but this handled goods traffic only. The first railway to carry passengers was the Oystermouth Railway which was authorised in 1804, and ran between Swansea and Mumbles, but that too boasted nothing more advanced in the way of motive power than horses.

As a result of George Stephenson's advice, the Stockton & Darlington Railway sought permission in its second Act of Parliament for the use of steam locomotives. So after *Locomotion* had been unloaded at Aycliffe Lane (now Heighington) from the horse-drawn carriages that had brought it from Newcastle it became the first steam locomotive to be operated on a public railway.

Two days after *Locomotion's* first journey under steam on their railway, the Stockton & Darlington advertised that the formal opening of the line would take place in 8 days time. Although several other Stephenson locomotives of the same general type had been operating successfully on the private Hetton Colliery Railway not many miles away, the inaugural steam-hauled train on 27 September 1825 created a lot of interest. *Locomotion* herself took over the first train at Shildon, since over the most westerly section of the line stationary steam engines were used because of the steep gradients, with horse traction over a short stretch between the Etherley and Brusselton Inclines. Various guests were invited to travel on the train from Shildon onwards, and as the railway's one passenger coach only held a comparatively small number of people, most of those with tickets had to be content with travelling in ordinary goods wagons. Others without tickets also quickly got in on the act, and by the time the train reached Stockton it was estimated there were something like 600 passengers aboard.

After this triumphal start, however, passengers on the Stockton & Darlington Railway were carried by private contractors using their own coaches hauled by horses, and it was not until 1833 that the railway company took over the operation of this form of traffic itself, and introduced regular steam-hauled passenger trains. It was the Liverpool & Manchester Railway, also engineered by George Stephenson, and opened in 1830, which was the first line to use locomotives for passengers and goods from the start, and Lancashire can thus claim to have had the first steam-worked railway. *Locomotion's* inaugural journey on 27 September 1825 can, however, be clearly seen as a significant landmark in the development of the Railway Age, and this event has rightly

George & Robert Stephenson Lucas
Science Museum

Locomotion v. Stage Coach

Frank Graham, Newcastle. Painter—Embleton

been celebrated in appropriate fashion after the passage of each subsequent period of 50 years.

Although we can now see, with the benefit of hindsight, the part the railways were to play in the development of our economy during the following century, what did the opening of the Stockton & Darlington Railway mean to those living in North-East England in 1825? First and foremost it enabled a far greater quantity of coal and other merchandise to be handled than previously. Roads in 1825 were very bad indeed, and even the turnpikes were churned into mud by the rains of the winter months. A horse on the railway could haul 12 tons of coal compared with a mere ton on the roads or about half of this as a pack-animal. After the Stockton & Darlington Railway had invented the "Dandy Cart" in 1828, which enabled the horses to ride in comfort on the down-hill stretches, they were able to get 240 miles a week out of each animal, a figure completely unheard of on the roads.

As a result of this easier and cheaper transport, traffic boomed, and over the first few years of the railway's existence, one of its main problems was learning how to manage this totally new sort of commercial enterprise. The first 168 tons of coal for shipment reached Stockton in January 1826, and in 1828 this business had increased to nearly 20,000 tons. Seven years later the total was 10 times this figure. With this rapid rise in coal traffic there was inevitably a massive expansion in trade generally, which benefitted everyone in the area either directly or indirectly. Not least were those whose agricultural, rather than industrial, produce could be conveyed cheaply to new markets, to their advantage as well as the purchasers'.

Although the Industrial Revolution started before the coming of the railways, it was the latters' contribution which changed England from a peasant economy to the leading world power, inside a century. It was the first significant step along this path that took place on 27 September 1825, and it is this event which is the subject of our 150th anniversary celebrations this year. **© 75**

Shildon Works

by K. W. Ashberry

Now one of the largest railway wagon building centres in Europe, Shildon Works has travelled far from the days when it consisted of the small engine shops of the Stockton & Darlington Railway 150 years ago.

Here, in fact, was the cradle of the steam locomotive, its coming surely one of the greatest events in the industrial revolution. For Timothy Hackworth, first locomotive engineer of the Railway, demonstrated the undoubted superiority of the locomotive over other forms of traction with his building of the "Royal George" at Shildon in 1827 and other successful designs.

The first workshops consisted of a narrow barn-like building divided into a joiners' and a blacksmiths' shop together with a small engine shed which could house two locomotives. Staff numbered 20 and increased by 50 by the time "Royal George" was built.

Shildon Works started to develop into the present works during the years 1833 to 34 but all that now remains of the original buildings is one known as the "long shed" now used as a wagon repair shop.

After working for the Railway Company for 8 years, Hackworth resigned to spend more time on his own business, which he had built up at the nearby Soho Works from 1833. The works were sold to the Stockton & Darlington on his death in 1850. In 1883 the Soho Works were closed and the work and men transferred to Shildon Works which by 1894 employed 500 men.

The remains of the Soho Works can be seen alongside the now restored Timothy Hackworth's cottage about ½ mile east from the present Works.

The Stockton & Darlington Railway had amalgamated with the North Eastern Railway in 1863, by which time the Darlington North Road Works had been

B.R.E.L./Simister

built, and eventually took over the building and repair of locomotives while Shildon concentrated on the building and repair of wagons.

In 1923 the London & North Eastern Railway, one of the four main groups formed under the railway amalgamation, took control of Shildon Works. When the adjoining locomotive sheds were taken over they were equipped for the concentration of wagon repairs. New shops were also built in the late 1940's. The first of January 1948 saw the nationalisation of the railways and Shildon Works then came under the control of the Chief Mechanical and Electrical Engineer of the E. & N.E. Regions until concentration of all Works under a central management took place in 1962. This separate Workshops Division with its own General Manager was seen necessary to develop a modernisation and rationalisation plan for the Workshops. Much of their equipment was old and obsolescent and under-used. The change-over from steam to diesel traction also altered requirements and tradional forms of work. Announced shortly afterwards the 5 year Workshop Plan provided for the closure of 15 of the 31 main works and the modernisation and re-equipment of the remaining 16 at a cost of £17 million, together with the rationalisation of the activities of these continuing works. Shildon survived and became one of the two main wagon building Works under the plan.

The 1968 Transport Act allowed all the Railway Works to manufacture rolling stock and general engineering products for private customers at home and abroad in addition to their traditional railway work and a wholly-owned subsidiary company of British Railways Board was formed, known as British Rail Engineering Limited, to exploit this new situation.

Shildon, modernised and efficient, was well placed to take advantage of these new powers and was the first BREL Works to build an export order, consisting of 150 covered vans for the Malayan Railway. Shildon's "bread & butter" has, however, been the building of thousands of high capacity coal wagons for the Central Electricity Generating Board merry-go-round services running from mine to power station all over the country, and also many of the latest types of wagons for British Rail.

The Works also builds specialised wagons for private customers and valuable orders have been completed for aggregate and cement wagons. There is a regular work load on rebodying wagons and conversions for vacuum brake working while over 30,000 wagons are repaired each year.

There are now 2,600 staff employed in this modern compact works who are proud of the traditions and skills they have inherited and the modern sophisticated wagons they build.

50 Ton Aggregate Wagon built at B.R.E.L. Shildon 1973. Exhibit No. 04.

In the distinctive Wedgwood Blue and Imperial Crimson livery of the Tilling Construction Group, this wagon is one of a fleet of 33 privately owned wagons built at Shildon in 1973 for the transfer of aggregate from the quarry to roadstone plants, the first of which was on the quayside at Hull, in an ideal position to serve the needs of the new Humber Bridge and associated road works. The wagon has a completely smooth interior to the two hoppers, and the air operated "clam-shell" doors permit continuous control of the rate of discharge at the terminal, where conveyor belts carry the stone direct to the grading plant.

50 Ton Wagon (Tilcon)

Covered Wagon B.R.E.L.

40 Ton Gross Laden Weight Covered Van Built at British Rail Engineering Ltd Shildon Works 1975
Exhibit No. 03.

British Rail are improving and expanding their national network of fast, direct freight services for single wagonload traffic between important traffic centres throughout the country, offering guaranteed overnight arrival. As a result existing customers are putting to rail a greater share of their traffic, and new traffic attracted to the services continues to increase. The service is being operated by three types of newly designed air braked covered vans, capable of up to 75 m.p.h. running, and 300 are currently being built at Shildon. The vans have full side access to speed loading and discharging, and the strengthened floor permits fork-lift trucks to operate freely in the vehicle.

46 Ton Gross Laden Weight High Capacity Coal Wagon Built at British Rail Engineering Ltd Shildon Works 1975
Exhibit No. 02.

One of 7,600 similar wagons built at Shildon over the last 10 years for use on "Merry-go-Round" services carrying coal between collieries and power stations in various parts of the country. Some 60% of the coal and coke traffic originating in the Eastern Region of British Rail is now carried in these wagons, with an annual

High Capacity Coal Waggon

tonnage of approximately 25 million, or half a million tons a week, over an average journey length of 35 miles. Merry-go-Round traffic is worked in trains of 30 wagons, having bottom doors automatically opened and closed by fixed lineside equipment at the power station, and hauled by locomotives fitted with special slow speed control, which permits the trains to be loaded and unloaded while moving at half a mile per hour through the terminals. The system thus permits a very high level of utilisation of wagons, locomotives and train crews. ©75

B.R.E.L. Exhibit No. 01. EXHIBITION STAND

Even a major railway Exhibition as comprehensive as RAIL 150 cannot do full justice to the range of work and skills developed in the Railway Workshops over the last 150 years. We have therefore brought together a valuable collection of models, old and new, from the various famous Works that together make up British Rail Engineering Ltd. The models, many of them made by Apprentices, and all of them by railwaymen, represent in miniature some of the outstanding contributions, past and present, that the Works have made to railways, in the form of locomotives, carriages and wagons.

Working on Royal George Model B.R.E.L.

List of Models

Covered G.A.S. Wagon (Built for Yugoslav Railways)	*Ashford Works*
"Duke of Gloucester"	*Crewe Works*
High Speed Train Power Car	*Crewe Works*
B.K. Type Container	*Derby Litchurch Lane Works*
16 Ton All Steel Mineral Wagon	*Derby Litchurch Lane Works*
Midland Compound	*Derby Locomotive Works*
Class 45 Diesel-Electric Locomotive	*Derby Locomotive Works*
Y25, B10 & BX1 Modern Freight & Passenger Bogies	*Derby Locomotive Works*
"Flying Scotsman"	*Doncaster Works*
Southern Region 0-6-0	*Eastleigh Works*
Traverser & Coach	*Glasgow Works*
"Royal George"	*Shildon Works*
26 Ton High Capacity Wagon	*Shildon Works*
Diesel-Hydraulic Loco	*Swindon Works*
Passenger Brake Van	*Wolverton Works*
6 Wheel Coach	*York Works*

G.P.O. EXHIBITION

Exhibit No. 127. Post Sorting Carriage.

Birth of the railways heralded an era of excitement and expansion for Britain's Postal Service. Histories of both networks have been closely "coupled" over the years. Today, three-quarters of post is carried at some stage by train.

The Post Office quickly grasped the advantages of speed and security which early railways held over mail coaches. In 1838, a "travelling post office" was introduced on the Grand Junction Railway, so mail could be sorted *en route.* Ingenious apparatus picked up and off-loaded bags while the train was moving—a system which became obsolete only in recent years.

The modern Post Office controls some 200 trains, notably "TPOs"—night mail trains that are the backbone of the system.

A sorting carriage from one of these is forming a centrepiece to the Post Office display at Rail 150. This is believed the first time such a coach has been made available for public inspection.

Another "first"—the issue, on August 13, of four stamps featuring locomotives spanning the railway age. They show Stephenson's "Locomotion" (at 7p); a North British Railway Drummond Waverley Class (8p); the Great Western's Caerphilly Castle (10p); and a new high-speed train (12p). This is the first railway set to be issued in Britain, which introduced both railways and stamps.

Postal souvenirs and collector's "pieces", including commemorative envelopes and presentation packs containing the stamps, can be purchased at the display. Items posted in a special box in the sorting carriaged will be marked with a commemorative hand-stamp prepared by the Shildon Jubilee Committee.

A replica of a 1910 road mailvan has been scheduled to tour the area, and postmen in historical uniform are being drafted in to help add extra colour to the scene.

N.U.R.

(formerly the Amalgamated Society of Railway Servants)—Exhibition stand and display. Exhibit No. 05.

The stand includes pictures showing the human side of railways, historical documents, badges and photographs of personalities. It tells the story of the N.U.R.'s fight to preserve the railway system. The organisation which resulted from the N.U.R. campaign—Transport 2000—is prominently featured.

The story of railways is the story of railwaymen. The full history of railwaymen since the Stockton & Darlington era is told in a unique book, in very limited supply. Only a few libraries have it and it is on sale only through the exhibition. It is written by a prominent lecturer and full details of the sources of information are given. Shorter versions are also available.

The background to the N.U.R. exhibition is a unique trade union banner. Probably one of the very earliest still preserved—it was originally made in the 19th century—it should be of special interest to those connected with the Trade Union and Labour Movements.

Restoration & Preservation of Locomotives

Maurice Burns

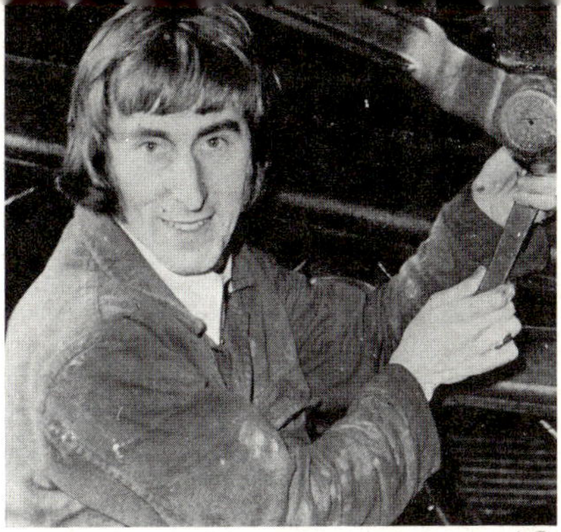

A.B.

Locomotive and railway preservation first started as far back as 1951 when a small group of enthusiasts wanted to save the closed, narrow gauge, Talyllyn Railway in Wales. This group of people who came from all walks of life formed themselves into a very effective amateur team called Talyllyn Preservation Society, who, over the years, became very professional in all aspects of operating a complete steam railway. Needless to say the Talyllyn Railway is a success but that early band of hopefuls could hardly have foreseen the mushrooming of their small beginnings into a national—even international—movement.

With railway preservation now in its 25th year it is particularly appropriate that this should coincide with the 150th Anniversary of the Stockton and Darlington Railway. From those very small beginnings there are now over 500 organisations, run by people dedicated to the age of steam.

The major upsurge in locomotive preservation has perhaps been brought about by the closure of so many lines in the 1960s under the Beeching Axe and with dieselisation of the National Railway system, the very last British Rail steam locomotive being withdrawn from service in 1968.

Whilst the first standard gauge locomotive to be preserved in working order was a small Great Northern Saddletank—still working to this very day—preservation was really made known to the masses by the saving from the breaker's yard of the famous L.N.E.R. Pacific No. 4472 "Flying Scotsman" for working enthusiasts' specials. After careful restoration to its former glory of L.N.E.R. Apple Green livery, this engine worked in all parts of the country bringing back nostalgic

K1 62005 "Before" restoration N.E.L.P.G.

memories of the rhythm, sounds and even smell of steam, to all those who treasured the days of old. Even the younger generation who only know the Diesels of today look on with a sense of excitement as this steam giant from years ago, roars past in a flash of shining steel.

This was just the beginning, for with the demise of steam in this country in the 1960's small groups of enthusiasts of all ages and from different walks of life, formed themselves into effective preservation groups to save particular classes of engines from extinction. In the early days most of these groups struggled to raise support, whether it was by collecting donations or selling items of railway interest, but railway preservationists, a breed of very determined people who despite the odds, never give in.

A typical engine may cost over £5,000 and possibly an equal amount to restore to working order. There are also many years of hard work learning the skills that are so quickly disappearing, working often in dirty, not ideal conditions and frequently without sufficient tools—preserving locomotives is not for the faint hearted.

Even when fully restored this is not the end of the work, for steam engines are in constant need of attention whether it be retubing a boiler, remetalling bearings or just simply repainting, and to meet the costs of these very expensive items all societies have sales teams which visit exhibitions like Shildon, selling a variety of goods to cater for all tastes—all the profits from which are used to keep their particular engine in steam.

The "Rail 150" Exhibition is indeed a fitting tribute to those preservation societies, for had it not been for their grit and determination a great part of our railway heritage would have been lost for ever and the fine collection of historic steam locomotives assembled for these celebrations would not have been at all possible.

In 1975 locomotive preservation has a full head of steam. Please help us to keep it that way by supporting the societies displaying engines today.

Acknowledgements

The success of the 150th Anniversary Celebrations of the Stockton & Darlington Railway has been made possible by the help and co-operation afforded to us from sources too numerous to mention individually.

However, it would be quite wrong of us to omit the grateful thanks of the organisers to all those who have helped in so many ways.

We have received unstinted support from Local Authorities; British Rail; the Railway Unions; the National Coal Board; the British Steel Corporation; Durham University; the Engineering Industry Training Board, and other public bodies, together with a large section of industry. To them, we extend our appreciation for both financial and material assistance.

We are also deeply indebted to the many individuals who have given their time and labour without thought of renumeration, in the knowledge that their enthusiasm and work has ensured the succes of this unique event.

Joint Committee,
Stockton & Darlington Railway,
150 Celebrations

No. 2005 After restoration at Grosmont, N.Y.M.R. N.E.L.P.G. M. Burns

Selection of Stock for Rail 150 Exhibition Cavalcade

The first meeting to discuss the possibility of holding a celebration to commemorate the 150th Anniversary of the Stockton & Darlington Railway was held in Middlesbrough in 1971. At that early stage we did not consider the possibility of a Cavalcade similar to that held in 1925 as British Rail would not allow steam operation on their lines. Fortunately this policy has since relaxed.

The final selection of locomotives was, in many cases, governed by factors outside the control of the Shildon Working Party of the Promotions Sub-Committee. The actual selection of available engines raised problems. Were engines, whether steam, diesel or electric, to be selected to show the historical and technical development of the railway engine? Should they have as many links as possible with engines appearing in 1925? Or should they demonstrate the different varieties of engines such as passenger, goods, shunting and industrial? In the end we decided to combine as many of these factors as we could with the added proviso that as many engines as possible should be capable of running in the Cavalcade. We were, however, working within the strict limitations laid down in our own budget; moving an engine across the country is not cheap.

When a provisional list was drawn up we found our difficulties were only just beginning. Some historically important engines like "Wylam Dilly", "Lion" of the Liverpool and Manchester Railway, were immobile in their museums because of their location in their buildings. Others like the Garret "William Francis" were mechanically awkward to move, besides involving costly road haulage. Again, other engines were needed to operate the basic services on the various preserved railways at the height of their summer season. Occasionally an engine, such as "Henry Oakley", which had not been used for years would suddenly reveal unexpected faults on close inspection, but in many cases these were overcome by hard work on the part of all concerned.

M. Wheeler Miss K. Hunter

Conditions were very different in 1925 when the steam engine was in every day use, complete with the backup facilities of large railway workshops. Now the restoration of railway engines is largely the work of volunteers working in their own spare time. Without their generous help, and the co-operation of the National Railway Museum, British Rail, the various independent railway companies and private locomotive owners, and the financial support, in a time of stringency, by the County Councils of Durham and Cleveland, this Celebration could never have been staged.

Michael Wheeler, *Chairman, Promotions Sub-Committee*

Assembling the Exhibition

by George Hinchcliffe

In general, British Rail will only move engines in steam if they are in first class condition, and are engines that once ran in regular service on B.R. tracks. They do not normally move industrial engines or vintage engines in steam.

In this day and age of diesel and electric trains, the movement of one steam locomotive over British Railways tracks involves a large number of personnel out of proportion to the size of the move.

First, the Chief Mechanical Engineer must satisfy himself that the locomotive is in a fit mechanical state, and that the boiler is sound. The operating staff must be sure the locomotive can move over the route without fouling bridges, platforms, etc., and not be too heavy for the track. The motive power officers along the line must be sure they can provide an experienced driver, fireman and inspector to operate the locomotive. The locomotive owner or trustee has to produce a boiler insurance certificate, and arrange insurance for physical damage, in case of a mishap, and public liability for £1 ¼ million.

Once the locomotives for the Exhibition and Cavalcade had been chosen by the Stockton & Darlington Committee, the principle of moving them and operating in the Cavalcade is the same for many as for one, but in this case there are several additional features. First, Flying Scotsman Enterprises arranged their own inspection

Bill Harvey "Inspector" Lightning Studios

by Mr. Bill Harvey, a locomotive engineman with many years experience on British Rail. He examined all the locomotives, and assessed their mechanical condition and their probability of being steamed and run in the Cavalcade. About ten engines already on the British Railway Board's approved list of locomotives, such as *Green Arrow, Leander,* and *Flying Scotsman* have a regular inspection by British Rail, and were not inspected by Mr. Harvey.

Most of the locomotives are not difficult to examine with the eventual aim of steaming. Many are regularly steamed or are in the process of restoration. A few locomotives are stripped down for overhaul, and therefore must wait until they are assembled before they can be examined. Most dedicated restorationists work hard and with enthusiasm to prepare their engines for Shildon.

The most interesting, and by far the most difficult to examine and assess, are engines which form part of the National Collection, and have not steamed, or even been moved, for many years. *Stirling No. 1* and *Henry Oakley* have been in York for many years. Great care must be taken to be sure no harm comes to these engines.

If an engine has been standing many years various fittings must be examined and overhauled. Injectors, water gauges, clack valves and the regulator valve are all cleaned and put in working order. Once this has been done the boiler is washed out and then fired up, the moving parts oiled, and everyone hopes for the best when the regulator is opened.

While all this is going on the essential administrative work, such as arranging insurance for the whole project, ordering coal and lubricants, making sure water is available on the route at selected points, and keeping the owners or trustees informed of progress goes ahed. There are frequent consultations with officers from British Rail.

Some of the smaller engines have been selected to operate a short distance passenger service we call the "Shildon Shuttle". This runs for about ¾ mile on British Rail Engineering Ltd., tracks to the East of the main exhibition site. Visitors who get very little opportunity to ride behind steam engines will enjoy this trip. One interesting feature will be the use of an engine at each end of the train.

The Grand Cavalcade is only the second to run this century. The last was in 1925 for the 100th Anniversary of the Stockton & Darlington Railway. Several engines which ran in the last Cavalcade will run in this one. In deciding which locomotives shall take part, several conditions particularly applicable to the vintage engines have been laid down. The engines must be capable of moving the four miles there and four miles back, they must have sufficient brake power to stop at short notice, there must be a crew who have sufficient experience to handle the engine. Having laid down these conditions, precautions will be taken and regulations for the conduct of the Cavalcade laid down. There will be an emergency water supply, radio communications with engines and base, markers at pre-determined intervals to ensure that engines are the correct distance apart, and the Shildon Crane in steam to take care of any total failure or a derailment. Fortunately, steam engines are simple, reliable machines, and very little is expected to be other than normal.

Once the Cavalcade is over, the approved engines, which run fairly regularly, will proceed to Darlington and be stored for a few hours and serviced before leaving in ones, twos and threes for their home base. The rest of the locomotives will return to Shildon to have their fires dropped, smokeboxes cleaned and then either wait for a towing locomotive or be loaded almost straight away on road vehicles to return home.

More than a year's planning and staging will all be over, and the project cleared in 24 hours.

Early Locomotives & Rolling Stock

A.B.

by M.G. Satow

The appearance of a full size working replica of 'LOCOMOTION', the No. 1 engine of the Stockton & Darlington Railway, marks the culmination of a co-operative effort by a group of engineering training establishments, companies and individuals in the North East of England. The replica is owned by 'The Locomotion Trust' established to promote, inter alia, " . . . the participation by firms, individuals and training establishments in the design, manufacture and operation of the said locomotive—to achieve maximum educational value from the project' and

Locomotion Steaming Trials

Locomotion Trust

' . . . the locomotive shall be preserved and maintained . . . as a live testimony to the commercial and technical enterprise of the North East of England in the early days of the railways of the world . . . '. It is, in short, a tangible memorial to the pioneers and has been constructed as part of the training of a future generation of engineers. Industry has generously contributed the materials and has assisted with work beyond the capacity of training establishments.

The original No. 1 engine, though preserved, could not be made to work again without such extensive rebuilding as to destroy its authenticity as a museum piece. In building the replica it has been necessary to compromise between the materials and techniques of 1825 and the needs of 1975 in terms of training, skills, materials and safety in operation. No secret is made of the fact that the art of the blacksmith has yielded to that of the welder and machinist, that the boiler is internally strengthened and improved in performance, that springs have been added to the axleboxes and the geometry of the 'parallel motion' improved. But, with these and other concessions to efficiency and to-day's safety requirements, the principles remain unaltered and the locomotive is essentially what George Stephenson set out to produce in 1825.

Forcett Coach M. Wheeler

The original was built with no more than a simple diagram, there were no working drawings. About a hundred drawings, based on measurements of the original, were produced by one training establishment, and the fabrication of parts and components was then undertaken by engineering training establishments from the Tees to the Tyne and from Bishop Auckland to the coast. Three 'generations' of apprentices have participated in the course of something over two years since the inception of the project.

	Original	Replica
Boiler	unstayed, Wrought Iron Rivetted	Internal stays, M.S. Welded
Grate area	8 sq. ft.	7.2 sq. ft.
Heated surface	52 sq. ft.	70 sq. ft.
Pressure lb/sq."	25-50	50
Cylinders Stroke	24"	24"
Bore	9" (later 10")	9"
Wheels, plug	4' 0" cast iron	4' 0" cast steel
Springs	NIL	3 blade laminated
Valve gear	loose eccentric, hand reversing	Loose eccentric hand reversing

Exhibit No. 12.
Railway Co. S. & D. Railway.
Coach No. 179.
Coach Type: 2 axle.
Name: Forcett Coach.
Normally exhibited to the public at North of England Open Air Museum, Beamish.

Although the Stockton & Darlington Railway was amalgamated with the North Eastern Railway in 1863, it retained a considerable measure of independence under a separate committee for a further ten years. Its independence included a separate locomotive and rolling stock establishment.

This carriage was built at the Hope Town Works, Darlington, of the Stockton & Darlington Railway in July, 1867, the external framework of the body being typical of Stockton & Darlington third class carriages of that period. However, most of the third class carriages of the 1860s were longer, and had six compartments. The seats in this carriage originally had no padding, but cushions were provided in the 1870s, and, at about the same time, the central partition seems to have been extended to the roof. It is not known when the handbrake and the 'porthole' windows in the ends of the carriage were provided. The Stockton & Darlington Railway number of the carriage was '179' but it was renumbered '1743' in the North Eastern Railway stock list in 1876.

In December, 1884, the Forcett Limestone Co. bought the carriage for £35, and it remained on the Forcett Railway, near Darlington, for about forty years, until it was placed in the Railway Museum, at York. It was eventually transferred to the North of England Open Air Museum, at Beamish, Co. Durham. Damage received during its later years in store at Clay Cross necessitated a complete restoration, and this has been carried out by volunteers among the staff at the Shildon works of British Rail Engineering Ltd. in 1974/75.

The livery of the restored carriage is based on a Stockton & Darlington Railway painting specification, dated 1859, which seems to have remained valid at least until c.1870. The letters and numerals are copies of the original markings, of which extensive traces were found during the work of restoration.

J.F.

Chaldron Wagon N. & E. Mining Inst. Northumberland Records Office

Exhibit No. 13.
Chaldron Wagon.
Normally exhibited to the public at North of England Open Air Museum, Beamish.

Chaldron Wagons or Black Wagons have a very long ancestry on railways and wagon ways in the North East. Unfortunately there are no drawings or description of the mid seventeenth century wagons. The earliest sketch is one of 1724. Two varieties are known, one hopper shaped, like the present examples, and the other with a vertical rear end. These wagons were designed to hold one chaldron of coal (53 cwt.), and originally had wooden wheels but these had been replaced by iron ones by the 1780s. At the time of the construction of the Stockton & Darlington railway these wagons were universal and indeed remained in common usage until this century. Indeed they are the ancestor of the present day mineral truck. The present examples were probably constructed in the 1870s. One chaldron wagon from Seaham is to be found in the Royal Scottish Museum collection and are of very slightly differing pattern, from the Stockton & Darlington Railway is in the National Railway Museum collection, together with two from the Seaham Harbour and Londonderry systems.

M.W.

Exhibit No. 14.
Date 1871.
Railway Co.: Dorking Greystone Lime Co.
Loco Type: 0-4-0.
Loco Class: Vertical Boiler.
Normally exhibited to the public at North of England Open Air Museum, Beamish.

This type of engine, with its vertical boiler, normally used by industrial concerns only, obtains its nickname from its resemblance to the machines to be found in catering establishments. Several other firms, like the Wintons of North Wales, constructed engines of a somewhat similar layout and often the smaller crane locomotives or steam tram engines had boilers of a similar type. Two other engines built by Head Wrightson were at work at Seaham Harbour, Co. Durham, until recent years, and one may be seen at Preston Hall Museum, Stockton on Tees. This particular locomotive spent all its working life until its withdrawal in 1939 at the Dorking Greystone Lime Co. quarry near Batchworth, Surrey.

M.W.

"Coffee Pot" & Chaldron Wagon

North of England Open Air Museum

Express Passenger Locomotives

Exhibit No. 21.
Date 1870. Railway Co.: G.N.R.
Loco Type: 4-2-2.
Loco. Class: Stirling Single. Loco No. 1.
Normally exhibited to the public at National Railway Museum, York.

Patrick Stirling, one of three brothers who were all locomotive engineers, succeeded Archibald Sturrock as the Great Northern Railway's Chief Engineer in 1866. He reigned in that position until his death in 1895 at the age of seventy-five years and giving no indications of retiring!

In 1870, Stirling produced his 'eight footer' which is considered by many to be the most graceful locomotive ever built. This is reflected in the sweeping curves of the smokebox which continue downwards to embrace the cylinders, and in the more sinuous curves of the running plate over the length of the locomotive. It should also be noticed that the top of the boiler is a long straight line without the customary steam dome.

The numerous 'eight footers' were still being built in 1895. The later lcomotives were some 50 per cent more powerful than the prototype and as such they remained in command of the principal East Coast expresses until after the turn of the Century. These locomotives took part in the railway races to the North in both 1888 and 1895. In that period the G.N.R. was said to be one of the fastest lines in the country.

No. 1 was withdrawn from service in 1907 and thus became one of the earliest locomotives to be preserved. It was last steamed in public in 1938 when some special trains were run in the London area. It also ran in the procession of the 1925 Centenary Celebrations of the Stockton & Darlington Railway.

The 'eight footer' could be considered as being representative of early East Coast express passenger motive power; the exhibition also contains the examples of the progression of steam power on this line spanning nearly seventy years, the others being *Henry Oakley, Flying Scotsman* and *Sir Nigel Gresley.*

The locomotive is shown in its original G.N.R. livery. No. 1 is one from the National Collection and is normally on display in the Museum at York.

K.A.L.

Stirling No. 1 R.C.T.S. Special

Photomatic Ltd.

L.N.W.R. No. 790 Hardwicke Derek Cross

Exhibit No. 22.
Date 1873.
Railway Co.: L.N.W.R.
Loco Type: 2-4-0.
Loco Class: Precedent.
Loco No. 790.
Loco Name: Hardwicke.
Normallly exhibited to the public at National Railway Museum, York.

This very successful engine is best known for its exploits in the famous railway races from London to Aberdeen in the summer of 1895. At this time there was intensive rivalry between the West Coast route (London & North Western Railway and the Caledonian Railway) and the East Coast route (Great Northern Railway, North Eastern Railway and the North British Railway). Normal travelling time for the 540 miles was 12 hours 20 minutes but the West Coast route won the "Race" in a record 8 hours 32 minutes—a record that has never been surpassed by steam.

"Hardwicke's" section was from Crewe to Carlisle in which she made 22 racing trips totalling 3,153 miles. Her finest performance was on 22nd August, covering the distance of 141 miles in 126 minutes, including the climb over the 915 feet summit of Shap at an average speed of 62.4 m.p.h. On this occasion, as before, her regular crew were Driver B. Robinson and Fireman W. Wolstencroft. It has often been said that these were exceptionally light trains, but "Hardwicke" was pulling 2.98 times its own weight compared with 2.73 on the famous run by L.M.S.R. "Princess Elizabeth" in 1936.

This engine was withdrawn from service in 1932 by the London, Midland & Scottish Railway. However, because of its historic past it was then preserved and repainted in the black livery of the London & North Western Railway. It has been prepared for steaming at Carnforth on behalf of the National Railway Museum.

M.W.

No. 990 Henry Oakley Photomatic

Exhibit No. 23.
Date 1898.
Railway Co.: G.N.R.
Loco Type: 4-4-2.
Loco Class U.
Loco No. 990.
Loco Name: Henry Oakley.
Normally exhibited to the public at National Railway Museum, York.

Two years after his appointment as Chief Engineer to the Great Northern Railway, Ivatt designed No. 990 as a successor to the Stirling singles and to fill a requirement for a more powerful locomotive to haul the heavy dining and sleeping car trains being introduced at that time on the East Coast main line.

Twenty-one of these locomotives were built and after being tested in service it was realised that a larger boiler would be of benefit. This was achieved and the 'Large' Atlantics appeared; it was expected that the smaller boilers would be replaced, but this was not to be and the small Atlantics were later superheated to improve their steaming capabilities. The addition of an extended smokebox to accommodate the superheater improved their outward appearance. No 990 is thus preserved in this condition.

These locomotives, when built, weighed 99 tons, and the closely spaced driving wheels are 6′ 8″ in diameter. The boiler supplied steam at 175 p.s.i. to the two 19″ diameter cylinders each of which has a separate set of valve gear.

No. 990 was withdrawn from service in 1937 and restored as seen today in G.N.R. livery. The last member of the class however survived the second world war and was not withdrawn until 1945. Only a handful of G.N.R. locomotives carried names, *Henry Oakley* being named after the General Manager.

Henry Oakley was one of the exhibits and ran in the procession of locomotives at the 1925 Stockton & Darlington Railway Centenary but was then in L.N.E.R. livery and numbered 3990. It was last steamed in public in 1953 on the occasion of another Centenary, that of the Doncaster Works where it was built.

This locomotive is one from the National Collection and is normally on display at the National Railway Museum in York.

K.A.L.

Exhibit No. 24.
Date 1902.
Railway Co.: Midland Railway.
Loco Type: 4-4-0.
Loco Class: Compound.
Loco No. 1000.
Normally exhibited to the public at National Railway Museum, York.

Compound expansion of steam on locomotives was an early attempt at conserving fuel. As applied to this particular design it was achieved by using the high-pressure steam from the boiler to drive the middle cylinder. The exhaust from this cylinder, which still contained useful energy, was then used to drive the two outside cylinders. Many experiments on compounding were carried out around the turn of the century and were relatively successful. Many railways built compound locomotives, but with an adequate supply of cheap coal the extra expense did not seem to be justified and many locomotives were rebuilt as simples, that is with normal cylinders and valves.

The Midland Railway No. 1000 was the first locomotive of this compound design, which eventually totalled some 240 engines, the final series being built well into L.M.S. days in 1932.

The "compounds" worked the main-line expresses over the whole of the Midland system and in L.M.S. days were used very successfully in Scotland. Inevitably they were replaced by more powerful locomotives and ended their days on secondary duties and semi-fast trains until the last member of the class was withdrawn from service in 1961.

M.R. No. 1000 was withdrawn from service in 1951 and was laid aside for many years awaiting a decision on its preservation. It was finally completely overhauled and restored at Derby and was returned to traffic in the summer of 1959 in the splendid original Crimson Lake livery as is seen today. It was used for a few years to haul special trains and then placed in the Museum of Transport at Clapham in London until it was moved to York in April 1975 in readiness for the opening of the National Railway Museum where it will again be on display to the public after the opening of the new Museum on 27th September.

K.A.L.

M.R. No. 1000 Compound (S.L.S. Special)

H. C. Casserley

Exhibit No. 25.
Date 1923.
Railway Co.: L.N.E.R.
Loco Type: 4-6-2.
Loco Class: A3.
Loco No. 4472.
Loco Name: Flying Scotsman.
Normally exhibited to the public at Carnforth Steam Centre.

This locomotive is considered by many to be the most famous of all. It was built early in 1923 shortly after the formation of the L.N.E.R. as No. 1472, the third of the new class of A1 Pacifics, and together with fifty one similar locomotives provided the L.N.E.R. with first class express motive power on its main lines. All the A1 locomotives were rebuilt to class A3 with higher pressure boilers and other improvements, and together with other new locomotives, this class eventually totalled seventy-eight. Each locomotive carried a name and most took their name from famous race horses.

The A3 class locomotive has the normal Gresley three-cylinder drive and valve gear, the boiler pressure is 220 pounds per square inch and the driving wheels are 6′ 8″ in diameter. In working order, the engine and tender weigh over 154 tons and the overall length is 70′ 5″.

No. 4472 Flying Scotsman S.R. Stock, Riccarton Junction A. M. Bowman

Various tenders were fitted to the class and the one seen on 4472 is a corridor tender holding 9 tons of coal and 5,450 gallons of water. The corridor running through the tender enabled the train crew of driver and fireman to be changed en route whilst working the non-stop trains between London and Edinburgh, a distance of 393 miles.

It was possible to pick up water whilst the train was in motion by means of a scoop situated beneath the tender and lowered into water filled troughs laid between the rails thus allowing greater distances to be covered without stopping for water, the tenderful of coal being sufficient for four hundred miles.

Flying Scotsman Eric Treacy

On the 1st of May 1928, No. 4472 hauled the first non-stop run of the "Flying Scotsman" from King's Cross to Edinburgh, departing at 10.00 am. 4472 had been named after this train, which still runs at the same departure time but is now hauled by a diesel-electric locomotive and stops additionally at Newcastle.

Flying Scotsman travelled 2,080,000 miles during its working life and was withdrawn from service on the 14th of January 1963 as British Railways No. 60103. It then carried a double chimney and German-type smoke-deflectors. Immediately after withdrawal, 4472 was restored to the condition as can be seen today.

Many famous drivers handled *Flying Scotsman* as she hauled trains on the East Coast main line, and in 1934, a speed of 100 miles per hour was achieved on a 1 in 200 down gradient with a test train. On the return journey, over 82 miles per hour was recorded whilst ascending the gradient.

Since preservation, *Flying Scotsman* has hauled many special trains and has been exhibited at many railway centres throughout the country. It may be recalled that in 1924 she was exhibited at the Wembley Exhibition in much the same condition as can be seen today. On May 1st 1968, then some 45 years old, *Flying Scotsman* repeated the non-stop run from London to Edinburgh; a creditable achievement for a locomotive in retirement.

In 1969, *Flying Scotsman* was completely overhauled and fitted with a bell and cowcatcher for an extensive North American tour and on its return to its native haunts it was again restored to the condition as seen today. The livery is that of the L.N.E.R. in the late 1920s; lined Apple Green.

The present owners are Flying Scotsman Enterprises Ltd., and the locomotive can be seen at various railway centres throughout the country.

K.A.L.

No. 6201 Princess Elizabeth climbing Shap Eric Treacy

Exhibit No. 26.
Railway Co.: L.M.S.
Loco Type: 4-6-2.
Loco Class: Princess Royal.
Loco No.: 6201.
Loco Name: Princess Elizabeth
Normally exhibited to the public at Ashchurch, Tewkesbury.

A product of the "thirties", when the prestige trains of all the four companies became faster, heavier and broke more records, No. 6201 is herself a world record holder. In 1936, she hauled a test train from London to Glasgow in 5 hours 52 minutes, and returned in 5 hours 44 minutes, at an average speed of over 70 m.p.h. for a total distance of 800 miles. Spectacular machines, the L.M.S. "Pacifics" were the rivals of those of the L.N.E.R., in the days when speed records were made and broken in rapid succession. The "Princess" class were not streamlined like the later "Pacifics", and looked rugged, powerful and fast. Their home ground was the West Coast main line, which contains as well as fast stretches, such severe gradients as Beattock and Shap, where the blast of their Caledonian-type hooters, as opposed to whistles, was in keeping with the wild country.

Mr. (later Sir) William Stanier came to the L.M.S. from the Great Western, at a time of locomotive crisis for the L.M.S. His "Pacifics", in their Crimson Lake livery contrasting with the Greens of the other companies, were the complete vindication of the L.M.S.'s choice of Chief Mechanical Engineer.

This locomotive was acquired by the Society in 1962, and was restored by them to its original state—a fine memorial to a great engineer.

A.P.

Exhibit No. 28.
Date 1937.
Railway Co.: L.N.E.R.
Loco Type: 4-6-2.
Loco Class: A4.
Loco No. 4498.
Loco Name: Sir Nigel Gresley.
Normally exhibited to the public on special excursion trains.

When built, No. 4498 was the 100th "Pacific" locomotive to be built to the designs of Mr. Gresley for the L.N.E.R. The A4s are a later development of the A3 class, and 35 locomotives of this class were designed and built to haul the fast non-stop trains between London and the Northern cities on the L.N.E.R. system.

No. 4498 Sir Nigel Gresley (Fully Streamlined) Photomatic

L.N.E.R. No. 4498 Sir Nigel Gresley
After restoration—Special Excursion crossing Smardale Viaduct

Alan Bowman

Mr. Gresley received a Knighthood in 1937 in recognition of his ability as an engineer and locomotive designer and hence this locomotive received its name *Sir Nigel Gresley* when built.

To enable the locomotive to achieve maximum efficiency when travelling at high speeds, the outer casing was streamlined, the front of the locomotive being styled on a French Bugatti petrol-driven railcar. A wedge shaped cab front, and side valances (since removed) added to the streamlining of the locomotive, the tender was also suitably blended with smooth lines to complete the effect.

The boiler can provide steam at 250 pounds per square inch and the 6′ 8″ diameter driving wheels are driven from three cylinders actuated by Gresley's derived valve motion. The locomotive and tender are 71 feet in length and weigh some 167 tons when in working order.

The tender is similar to that seen on *Flying Scotsman* and is also fitted with a corridor and water scoop. On the non-stop runs between London and Edinburgh, the locomotive crew were changed en route by passing through the corridor in the tender from their compartment in the leading coach of the train. The changeover point on these journeys was some eight miles north of York.

Apart from one locomotive of the class, which was damaged beyond repair during an air raid on York in 1942, the A4 locomotives were worked hard throughout their existence until the summer of 1966, when the surviving two locomotives were withdrawn from service and their places taken by the more modern diesel locomotives of today.

On the 3rd of July 1938, one member of the class, No. 4468 *Mallard* was driven at a speed of 126 miles per hour between Grantham and Peterborough, thus achieving a World record for steam traction which has never been broken. *Mallard* is also preserved in the National Railway Museum at York, and carries a plaque on the side of the streamlined casing to commemorate its record.

An example of the working of the A4 locomotives can be judged from records; they regularly worked trains weighing over 300 tons at an average speed of over 60 miles per hour for a distance of almost 400 miles. It is not unknown for one of these locomotives to perform such a duty and after a short servicing period to travel a similar distance thereby logging over 800 miles in one day.

Locomotives such as *Sir Nigel Gresley* were expected to travel some 75,000 miles between major overhauls for which they were normally returned to the works at Doncaster. Mileage records ceased to be kept after 1962, but it is estimated that *Sir Nigel* travelled some two million miles in revenue earning service. In 1957 whilst hauling a private excursion, No. 4498 attained a speed of 113 miles per hour on the same stretch of track where *Mallard* achieved her fame. This speed has never since been equalled by a steam locomotive. It is a fitting tribute to the preservation societies to record that in 1967, when in private ownership, No. 4498 hauled a special 385-ton train over the Shap incline in Westmorland in a faster time than had previously been recorded.

The attractive livery of L.N.E.R. Garter Blue is that used by that company when No. 4498 was built, although other locomotives of the class were turned out in either silver or lined-green liveries according to the type of train they were intended to haul. The silver locomotives were specially finished to match the silver-painted coaches of the "Silver Jubilee" train.

Sir Nigel Gresley is owned by the A4 Locomotive Society and whilst it is not on permanent display, it can be seen either working special trains or when it is visiting one of the various railway centres throughout the country.

K.A.L.

L.M.S. No. 5680 Leander at Dinting C. D. Pemberton

Exhibit No.
Date 1936.
Loco Class: Jubilee 4-6-0.
Loco No.: 5690. Loco Name: Leander
Normally on display to the public at the Dinting Railway Centre.

These famous "Jubilee" locomotives worked all over the L.M.S. system competently handling express passenger trains even on the difficult routes through the Pennines. They regularly worked into York and on occasion up the East Coast Main Line to Newcastle. They were withdrawn from service in 1962. The last of the three locomotives of this class to be preserved, "Leander" was purchased from Woodham's Bros. scrapyard, like so many others, and given a full general overhaul by the Derby works of British Rail Engineering for its new owners, the Stockport firm of Oliver, Taylor, Crossley & Co. After twelve months at Derby, this rustv hulk emerged in its resplendent maroon L.M.S. livery to be shown to the public at Derby Works Open Day in August 1973. Back in her old form, "Leander" justified her overhaul, working special trains between Guide Bridge and Sheffield, and later between Oxford and Hereford.

Exhibit No. 29. Date 1948.
Railway Co.: L.N.E.R./B.R.
Loco Type: 4-6-2.
Loco Class: A2.
Loco No. 532.
Loco Name: Blue Peter.
Normally exhibited to the public on special excursion trains.

Blue Peter is the sole surviving example of the designs of Arthur H. Peppercorn who, in succeeding Edward Thompson, became the last Chief Mechanical Engineer of the L.N.E.R. before Nationalisation in 1948. Before his retirement in 1946, Edward Thompson had designed and built three different designs of 4-6-2 locomotive all with radical departures from the earlier Gresley designs. Not all the detail changes were successful and on taking over from Thompson, Peppercorn made certain changes to the outstanding orders for building at Doncaster which resulted in this design. Fifteen locomotives were built, all of which retained a number of standard parts and subsequently a further design was produced (the A1s), but with larger driving wheels.

Whilst the design of this locomotive must be credited to the L.N.E.R., this locomotive was not delivered until the 25th March, 1948 and appeared as number 60532 with the tender lettered "British Railways". It was first allocated to York and remained there until 1949, working main line trains. After an overhaul at Doncaster, where some modifications were made, including the fitting of a double chimney, it was transferred to Scotland where it remained until its withdrawal from service on 31st December, 1966.

No. 532 Blue Peter at Hawick Alan Bowman

The A2 class locomotives were often to be seen working express trains on the coast route between Northallerton and Newcastle via Stockton and Hartlepool, and were well suited to working this route due to their high tractive effort. A similar situation existed on the Scottish route between Edinburgh and Aberdeen.

All the fifteen locomotives were named, the majority of them following the L.N.E.R. tradition of using the names of famous race horses. The name *Blue Peter,* whilst being derived from the International Code Flag 'P', used by vessels about to leave port was also the name of the 1939 Derby winner owned by Lord Rosebery. In that year, whilst winning the Derby and other races including the "2000 Guineas", *Blue Peter* earned almost £32,000 for its owner, more than enough to purchase three Doncaster Pacific locomotives at the time.

The locomotive *Blue Peter* weighs over 161 tons when in working order and is over 60 feet in length. The 6' 2" driving wheels are driven by three cylinders fed with steam generated in the boiler at 250 pounds per square inch. Each cylinder has its own set of valve gear.

After withdrawal from service, *Blue Peter* was stored in Scotland for more than a year pending sale to a private owner. On completion of the negotiations, *Blue Peter* returned south and was put into store at York where some restoration work was carried out by its new owners before being sent to Doncaster for overhaul and repainting.

Over 3000 people responded to an appeal for funds, largely because of the kindness shown by the producers of the

L.N.E.R. No. 532 Class A2 Blue Peter, Didcot

P. B. Whitehouse

B.B.C. T.V. programme of the same name in featuring the locomotive in their programme on several occasions. After completion of the work at Doncaster, when the locomotive was handed over to its new owners in resplendent condition, it received a tremendous reception from thousands of well wishers who heard about it on T.V.

Blue Peter is exhibited in the same livery as when built, that of L.N.E.R. Apple Green. The number 532 and the tender lettering "L.N.E.R." depict how it would have appeared had Nationalisation of railways been delayed by three months.

The locomotive is at present owned by Mr. G. Druery who appreciates the support of the Blue Peter Locomotive Society. It is not normally on display to the public but may be seen from time to time at various centres throughout the country, and also when occasionally hauling special trains on British Rail.

K.A.L.

Exhibit No. 30.
Date 1948.
Railway Co.: S.R./B.R.
Loco Type: 4-6-2.
Loco Class: Merchant Navy.
Loco No.: 35028.
Loco Name: Clan Line.
Normally exhibited to the public at Hereford.

This locomotive represents the ultimate design of passenger tender locomotives of the Southern Railway. It was designed by O. V. S. Bulleid who, from being a pupil at Doncaster Works, rose to become personal assistant to H. N. Gresley and took charge of locomotive design for the Southern Railway in 1937. The result was the "Merchant Navy" Class, which regularly hauled such famous trains as "Golden Arrow", "Night Ferry", Bournemouth Belle", and the "Atlantic Coast Express". Like Gresley, Bulleid was willing to try new ideas, and the "Merchant

No. 35028 Clan Line as built Photomatic

Navy" locomotives had many novel features including totally-encased chain–operated valve gear lubricated in an oil bath, an all-welded steel fire box, special wheels and an air-smoothed casing.

A number of these new features became excessively expensive to maintain so the class as a whole was rebuilt between 1956 and 1959. These locomotives, which were named after shipping lines were all withdrawn by 1967. When working enthusiast specials they have been over Shap and Aisgill to Carlisle also up the East Coast main line as far as Newcastle. This locomotive was purchased straight out of service and is now used to operate enthusiasts specials in various parts of the country. It is now housed at Hereford.

A.C./J.R.

No. 35028 Clan Line as rebuilt Peter Groom

Exhibit No. 31.
Date 1951.
Railway Co.: B.R.
Loco Type: 4-6-2.
Loco Class: Britannia.
Loco No.: 70000.
Loco Name: Britannia.
Normally exhibited to the public at Severn Valley Railway Co., Bridgnorth.

When the railways were Nationalised in 1948, the introduction of a series of standard locomotives was put in hand to replace the ageing classes of the old Companies. Under the direction of Mr. Riddles, all the old works and drawing offices had a hand in their design. The "Standards" were designed for efficiency and ease of maintenance and have, for example, all the valve gear outside and the wheels completely uncovered. The result in the "Britannia" class, the first of the standard engines, is certainly not ugly.

Reception of the "Brits" was mixed. Most enginemen appreciated the motives behind the design, and the attempts to increase their own working comfort, although the ex-G.W.R. men were not so happy; perhaps this was due to these engines' basic fault of not being a pure Swindon Product! East Anglia took well to them, with excellent results, and on the Southern Region they did very good work with the "Golden Arrow" Continental service. Most of the locomotives were named after famous Britons, and *William Shakespeare,* No. 700004, was exhibited at the 1951 Festival of Britain. Wherever needed, they ran with the famous engines of the old companies, and although they never turned out remarkable "one off" runs like the A3s, A4s, "Princesses" and "Kings", they were nonetheless fast and reliable. This locomotive was purchased privately, and moved to Bridgnorth for restoration by the Britannia Locomotive Society.

A.P.

B.R. No. 70000 Britannia at Bridgnorth

Colourviews

No. 32662 Terrier. L.C.G.B. Special Train

Photomatic

Exhibit No. 41.
Date 1872.
Railway co.: L.B. & S.C.R.
Loco Type: 0-6-0T.
Loco Class: A1X.
Loco No. 32636.
Loco Name: Fenchurch.
Normally exhibited to the public at—Bluebell Railway, Sheffield Park, Uckfield, Sussex.

Out of fifty engines built by Stroudley for the old London, Brighton and South Coast Railway, no less than ten surivive. They were built for light duties from 1872 onwards and their size and pleasing appearance made them ideal for preservation by the time the last one was withdrawn in 1963. One, indeed, has become a public house "sign" on Hayling Island, Hampshire, near the line on which some of these engines ran. Another one, "Waddon", has travelled far afield since it has been preserved and is now displayed in Montreal, at the Canadian Railroad Museum. Other examples of this class of locomotive may be seen at work on the Kent and East Sussex Railway and at Bressingham.

Fenchurch, itself, was built in 1872 and was the first of the class to enter service. Like other engines of the London, Brighton and South Coast Railway it was painted in yellow ochre, the famous "Stroudley's improved engine green". This engine was sold in 1898 to the Newhaven Harbour Company but reboilered to the A1/X classification at Brighton Works in 1913. In 1926 it was taken over by the Southern Railway and after this, until its withdrawal in 1964, was used on several branch lines in the South of England such as the Kent & East Sussex, and the Hayling Island Branch. During its lifetime, before withdrawal for preservation, it ran a total of 1,109,513 miles.

M.W.

Exhibit No. 42.
Date 1907.
Railway Co.: Caledonian Railway.
Loco Type: 0-4-4T.
Loco Class: 439.
Loco No.: 419.
Normally exhibited to the public at Scottish Railway Preservation Society, Falkirk.

No. 419 was one of a class of ninety-one locomotives built between 1900 and 1925, as a later development of this type of locomotive dating back to the 1884 designs of Dugald Drummond.

This two cylinder design with 5′ 9″ diameter driving wheels was extensively used on suburban services radiating from Glasgow Central Station until replaced by more powerful locomotives of L.M.S. design in the 1930s. The engines were then relegated to less arduous branch-line duties in most areas of Scotland until their final withdrawal in the 1960s. Locomotives of this type were also used for banking duties at Beattock, assisting heavy trains up the notorious incline to the summit.

In 1962, No. 419 was withdrawn from service and purchased by her present owners and restoration work carried out in Scotland. The pale blue livery is the one that the Caledonian Railway used on their locomotives prior to 1923, when that company was absorbed into the London Midland & Scottish Railway Co.

K.A.L.

Caledonian Railway No. 419 Derek Cross

No. 246 Morayshire

Derek Cross

Exhibit No. 43.
Date 1927.
Railway Co.: L.N.E.R.
Loco Type: 4-4-0.
Loco Class: D49.
Loco No.: 246.
Loco Name: Morayshire.
Not normally exhibited to the public at present.

At the time of the grouping of the railway companies in 1923, the L.N.E.R. inherited many ancient and varied classes of tender locomotives, few of which were considered capable of performing duties envisaged for the future policy of the new company. The D49 class were designed and built as one of the new classes introduced and while they were not unsuccessful in performing their duties, many of the older locomotives lingered for many years on lighter duties.

Before 1927, Mr. Gresley had confined the use of three-cylinders to the larger locomotives such as *Flying Scotsman,* but with the introduction of the D49 class, the three cylinder design became standard for passenger locomotives on the L.N.E.R.

Seventy-six locomotives were built of this design, about half of which were named after the counties through which the L.N.E.R. worked their traffic. Hence the name of this locomotive *Morayshire.* The remainder were named after famous Fox Hunter packs. The class were therefore known as "Shires" and "Hunts".

After short trial periods at various depots, these locomotives were put to work hauling semi-fast express trains over the Northern area of the L.N.E.R. and in Scotland. They were powerful and lively engines, and as very often happens, they were called upon for main line duties such as the Leeds-Glasgow Pullman trains via

Darlington as far as Newcastle. The D49s earned a reputation of 'rough riders' when travelling at speed and it is on record that when locomotive crews had progressed to this class, they received such a regular bruising that applications to return to shunting duties were not uncommon.

When the B1 class arrived in large numbers in early British Railways days, the "Shires" and "Hunts" were transferred to less onerous duties in country areas and, as well as passenger stopping trains, some of these locomotives were observed on freight and mineral work. Their fate was sealed by the introduction of diesel multiple units, and *Morayshire*, the last of the class in service, was withdrawn from service in Scotland in 1961 and purchased for preservation. The locomotive was restored to the 1928 livery of Apple Green as is seen today.

The three cylinder D49s had driving wheels of 6' 8" diameter and a boiler pressure of 180 pounds per square inch. The length of the locomotive and tender is some 58 feet, and in working order weighs approximately 65 tons.

Morayshire is owned by the Royal Scottish Museum and at the time of writing is not normally on display to the public.

K.A.L.

Exhibit No. 44.
Date 1936.
Railway Co. L.S.W.R./S.R.
Loco Type: 4-6-0.
Loco Class S15.
Loco No.: 841.
Loco Name: Greene King.
Normally exhibited to the public at Stour Valley Railway Chappel and Wakes Colne Station, Essex.

The S15 class was introduced by Urie for the London & South Western Railway as a mixed-traffic version of his express passenger 4-6-0s, which later became the "King Arthur" class. The Southern Railway built more similar engines, the second batch of which differed in various details from their earlier locomotives. No. 841 is one of the last batch, dating from 1936. Although designed primarily for parcels traffic with 5' 7" diameter wheels, the locomotives were frequently pressed into passenger service at peak holiday periods.

After withdrawal from service in 1964, No. 841 was rescued from the locomotive graveyard at Barry in September 1972. Considerable hard work by the Essex Locomotive Society has restored this locomotive to its present fine condition and it has been named *Greene King.*

P.W.B.S.

B.R. No. 30841

Peter Groom

Exhibit No. 45. **Date 1949.**
Railway Co.: G.W.R. **Loco Type: 4-6-0.**
Loco Class: Modified Hall.
Loco No.: 6960.
Loco Name: Raveningham Hall.
Normally exhibited to the public at Steamtown, Carnforth.

During the 1920s locomotives with four cylinders handled the majority of express passenger trains on the G.W.R. but 2 cylinder engines of the "Saint" class fitted with inside Stephenson link motion designed by Churchward proved exceptionally good runners. In Collett's day a decision was made to use this type of design for an improved mixed traffic engine capable of hauling heavier express trains at high speed and as a trial No. 2925 Saint Martin was rebuilt from a standard Saint engine, but having 6′ 0″ driving wheels insead of 6′ 8½″.

This engine proved so successful that it became the prototype of a new class, the "Halls", eventually to number 330. They differed from the rebuild inasmuch as they had 4½″ higher pitched boilers, modified frames and cylinders with outside steam pipes.

One of the notable runs performed by a member of the class was deputising on the "Bristolian" in an emergency and running to time throughout.

In 1946, due to the non-availability of the best grade of Welsh coal it was decided to convert several engines to oil burning and a number of Halls were converted and allocated to Laira shed, Plymouth. The fuel was carried in a 1950 gallon tank mounted in the tender and results proved highly satisfactory. Foreign currency, however, was not forthcoming to maintain supplies of oil in the quantity required and gradually these engines were reconverted to coal.

6960 "Raveningham Hall" was rescued from Barry in late 1972 and has been restored mainly by volunteer labour at Steamtown, Carnforth, new fibreglass boiler lagging and new cladding, a mechanical lubricator and two live steam injectors being fitted during the course of restoration. It is hoped that during 1976 the locomotive will once again travel over British Rail metals to either Barrow or Leeds and that the engine will be in steam on certain weekends during 1975, to be advised.

B.T.

G.W.R. Modified Hall No. 7920, Coney Hall Photomatic

Exhibit No.: 46.
Date 1930. **Railway Co.: G.W.R.**
Loco Type: 0-6-0.P.T.
Loco Class: 57XX.
Loco No. 7752.
Normally exhibited to the public at Birmingham Steam Museum.

These 0-6-0 pannier tanks of the Great Western Railway 57XX class reached a total of 863 locomotives in twenty years, replacing many obsolete and non-standard small tank locomotives. This made the class the most prolific on the G.W.R.

Due to good design they were found all over the Western system. Even after nationalisation only the former G.W.R. sheds at Truro, Abercynon, Treherbert, Aberystwyth and Machynlleth did not have an example of this class of locomotive.

Whilst these small tank locomotives may never receive the publicity of their bigger, named brothers, they were familiar to all who travelled by rail for holidays in areas served by the Great Western Railway. These were "the maids of all work" throughout the Great Western Railway. Several of these locomotives were still in good operational condition when the British Railways policy of dieselisation was completed. No. 7752 was sold to the London Passenger Transport Board to work on the electrified lines when the power was off and the commuters in bed.

This locomotive has the older design of G.W.R. cab as fitted to pannier tanks prior to 1940. The pannier tank arrangement for the water supply was peculiar to the Great Western Railway, being a development of the old saddle tank design. These tanks were easier to make and maintain. They fitted round the Belpair fire box used on this engine.

Locomotive No. 7752 had the honour of working the last steam train on a British public railway under official auspices, as L.P.T.B. No. L94 from Moorgate to Neasden on 6th July, 1971.

W.H.

No. 7752 at Tyseley P. B. Whitehouse

Exhibit No. 47. Date 1936.
Railway Co.: L.N.E.R. Loco Type: 2-6-2.
Loco Class: V2. Loco No.: 4771.
Loco Name: Green Arrow.
Normally exhibited to the public at Steamtown, Carnforth.

Five of these locomotives were built in 1936 as the fore-runners of a new class designed to meet the ever-increasing demands of the day for fast and reliable mixed traffic locomotives. This design embodied many of the successful features of earlier Gresley designs and many of the basic parts were modelled on the features of the A3 class.

The driving wheels of 6′ 2″ diameter, together with the efficient boiler and cylinder assembly, made these locomotives very popular for both express passenger and freight work. When built the first five locomotives were allocated to various depots as far apart as London and Dundee. They were put through extensive trials and No. 4771 could be regularly seen hauling the 3.55 p.m. "Scottish Goods" north from London and putting up a fine performance for this very heavy train. Other duties met with equal success especially in Scotland in the hilly regions where the V2s made light work on the main lines with the ever-increasing traffic demands. The prudent decision to build further numbers was quickly taken and at the outbreak of war almost one hundred of these locomotives were in service and further numbers were in the course of construction which continued until 1944. It was quickly realised that the V2s could work easily as well as the larger "Pacific" locomotives, they were dubbed by the L.N.E.R. crews as "the locomotives that won the war."

A total of 184 were built. A few were named after famous British Army regiments and two after northern public schools. *Green Arrow,* however, carried its name from the beginning, being derived from that of the special registered freight service that had recently been introduced.

Green Arrow on Fast Freight Photomatic

It is of interest to note that, when built, all the three cylinders and valve chests together with the smokebox saddle were all cast as a one-piece steel casting.

The V2s were to be found working on all main routes of the L.N.E.R. until their demise in the early 1960s when the new diesel-electric locomotives rendered them redundant. The three-cylindered V2 class were 66′ 5″ long and in working order weighed 144 tons.

On withdrawal from service, *Green Arrow* was completely overhauled and repainted in the L.N.E.R. livery of Apple Green as when built.

Green Arrow is one of the National Railway Museum collection of locomotives and rolling stock.

K.A.L.

No. 4771 Green Arrow Derek Cross

No. 7808 Cookham Manor and No. 6998 Burton Agnes Hall Dumbleton

No. 7808 Cookham Manor Dumbleton

Exhibit No. 48.
Date 1938.
Railway Co.: G.W.R.
Loco Type: 4-6-0.
Loco Class: Manor.
Loco No.: 7808.
Loco Name: Cookham Manor.
Normally exhibited to the public at Great Western Railway Society, Didcot.

These light-weight modern, two cylinder, passenger locomotives marked the completion of the final stage of the Great Western Railway standardisation policy of 4-6-0 type steam locomotives for passenger services.

In the 1960 period these locomotives were mostly based in the Welsh holiday areas around Oswestry, Machynlleth and Carmarthen, whilst others remained in the West Country for running and assisting heavy passenger and freight trains over the heavily-graded Devon and Cornwall lines.

Such important trains as the "Cambrian Coast Express" were in the 1950-60s entrusted to these locomotives with exemplary performances. The polished copper and brass and spotless paintwork of the "Manor" class locomotives allocated to Aberystwyth depot for the Cambrian Coast Express duties has now become legendary.

No. 7808 has been fully restored to its Great Western Railway livery and has been completely mechanically overhauled to the stringent requirements of British Railways authorities to permit it to operate under its own steam, on special trains on British Rail main lines. The locomotive is also accompanied by a fully-restored Great Western Railway train of the pre-war period.

W.H.

Exhibit No. 49. **Date 1947.**
Railway Co.: L.M.S.
Loco Type: 4-6-0.
Loco Class: 5M.T.
Loco No.: 4767.
Loco Name: George Stephenson.
Normally exhibited to the public at North Yorkshire Moors Railway, Grosmont.

Often described as the most successful engines built by the London Midland and Scottish Railway, the 842 examples of the Stanier-designed Class 5 4-6-0s were masters of their work whether it be on freight or express passenger duties. First introduced in 1934, they could soon be seen from London to the Highlands of Scotland. Shortly after the last war, the then Chief Mechanical Engineer of the L.M.S., Mr. H. G. Ivatt, decided that in order to keep these mixed traffic engines abreast of modern developments a new batch of engines should be built with the intention of lessening maintenance required between overhauls. To enable proper trials to be conducted, 30 new engines were built, some with the then new idea of "roller bearings" and differently designed valve gears, All previously built engines had Walschaerts valve gear, but for this experiment some engines were fitted with an Italian Caprotti valve motion and one engine, No. 4767, with Stephenson's valve gear, a design originally introduced by George Stephenson over 100 years previously!

Special cost records were to be kept to assess the relative merits of the different locomotives, but because of Nationalisation in 1948 the final results were never known. No. 4767 was unique in the fact that it was the last main line locomotive in England to be fitted with outside Stephenson's valve gear. Over the years the engine had a reputation of being stronger in acceleration or climbing against the grade than its sister engines, but because of the coming end of steam on British Rail, the engine was withdrawn from traffic in 1967. As No. 44767 the engine was purchased privately for preservation, and during 1975 has been completely overhauled and restored to its original L.M.S. livery as No. 4767, by members of the North Eastern Locomotive Preservation Group. It is quite fitting that this locomotive which carried the Stephenson Link Valve Gear should in 1975 be named after the most famous of all engineers "George Stephenson", by the Rt. Hon. William Whitelaw at the "Rail 150" Exhibition, to provide a lasting reminder of these 150th Anniversary Celebrations.

M.B.

L.M.S. No. 4767 Class 5 B.R.

L.N.E.R. No. 1306 Mayflower Eric Treacy

Exhibit No. 50.
Date 1948.
Railway Co.: L.N.E.R.
Type No.: 4-6-0.
Loco Class: B1.
Loco No.: 1306.
Loco Name: Mayflower.
Normally exhibited to the public at Steamtown, Carnforth.

Following the death of Sir Nigel Gresley in 1941, Edward Thompson was appointed as his successor and became only the second Chief Mechanical Engineer of the L.N.E.R. in eighteen years. At this crucial time in the second World War, evidence of detail weaknesses in the Gresley designs were becoming apparent, especially in the conjugated valve gear. In the main these were due to the reductions in maintenance standards being experienced. The demand for extra motive power to help with the heavy demands of wartime traffic was realised and to combat this need it was expected that the earlier Gresley designs would be perpetuated. Thompson however had strong reservations and successfully presented his case, outlining the weaknesses and also the special steels required by the Gresley designs.

The result of all this was the speedy creation of the B1 class which utilised many parts from earlier locomotives known for their reliability and performance. For example the boiler of the B17 class was used, the cylinders and valves of the K2s, the wheel centres of the V2 class and so on. The result was a clever synthesis of locomotive engineering which recognised the problems of the time.

Ten B1s were built in 1942, and a further four hundred between 1946 and 1948 by which time they were considered to be one of the new L.N.E.R. standard classes, replacing many locomotives which but for the war would have been withdrawn from service. Forty of the class were named after South African antelopes whilst others were named after L.N.E.R. directors of the time. The name *Mayflower,* now carried by this locomotive, was originally carried by its sister locomotive No. 61379.

The B1 class locomotive is a two-cylindered mixed traffic engine with 6′ 2″ diameter driving wheels. The boiler pressure is 225 pounds per square inch and in working order the locomotive and tender weigh 123 tons and are 61′ 7″ in length. The standard L.N.E.R. tender carries 7 ½ tons of coal and 4200 gallons of water.

No. 1306 entered service in green livery and spent most of its working life at Hull hauling both passenger and freight trains until the mid-1960's when it was transferred to the West Riding of Yorkshire, it was finally withdrawn from service from Low Moor depot near Bradford in 1967. This locomotive was originally saved by the B1 Society and is normally on display at Steamtown, Carnforth where its restoration is being undertaken.

K.A.L.

Exhibit No. 51.
Date 1949.
Railway Co.: L.M.S.
Loco Class: 2MT. **Loco Type: 8-6-0.**
Loco No.: 41241.
Normally exhibited to the public at Keighley and Worth Valley Railway.

This class was designed in 1946 as a "maid of all work" for branch line services, to replace a motley collection of locomotives which posed the twin problems of old age and lack of standardisation to the London Midland and Scottish Railway. By Nationalisation in 1948, thirty had been built, and British Railways built a further hundred. The B.R. Standard Class 8400, of which 30 were built, were of a very similar design.

Some of the class, unlike No. 41241, were equipped for "push-pull" working, where the engine was permanently at one end of the train, so doing away with the need for the locomotive to run around the train at the end of its journey.

The class was well distributed around the former L.M.S. system. After early service on the Somerset and Dorset line, No. 41241 moved to Skipton, Yorks., via Shropshire. Withdrawn in 1967, it was purchased by the Keighley and Worth Valley Railway, where it hauled the opening train, and has been the line's most used engine ever since. In fact it is still the steady revenue earner it was intended to be.

A.P.

No. 41241 Class 2 M.T. Derek Cross

Exhibit No. 52.
Date 1949.
Railway Co.: B.R.
Loco Type: 2-6-0.
Loco Class: K.1.
Loco. No.: 2005.
Normally exhibited to the public at North Yorkshire Moors Railway, Grosmont.

The class K1, first introduced in 1949, was a simplified development of Sir Nigel Gresley's three cylinder K4, which were especially built in 1937 for the arduous West Highland Line between Glasgow and Fort William. One of the six K4s was reconstructed in 1945 with just two outside cylinders to lessen maintenance, by Mr. E. Thompson the Chief Mechanical Engineer of the L.N.E.R. With the success of this experiment, Mr. A. H. Peppercorn who succeeded Mr. Thompson as C.M.E., ordered a new batch of 70 engines for mixed-traffic duties both in the Highlands of Scotland and throughout the eastern half of England.

Built entirely by the North British Locomotive Company Ltd. in Glasgow, the engines were constructed between 1949 and 1950, No. 2005 being out-shopped in June, 1949. Allocated entirely in the North East of England during her working life, 62005 has many claims to fame. In March 1965 she partnered the preserved K4 *The Great Marquess* on the last British Railways' steam passenger train over the former Whitby-Pickering Railway, part of which has now been taken over by the North Yorkshire Moors Historical Railway Trust and is now a thriving tourist attraction. No. 62005 also has a rare distinction amongst engines, of having beed used as a "Royal" engine when Her Majesty the Queen visited the North of England in both 1960 and again in 1967 — the year the engine was withdrawn from service.

Unlike the remaining engines in the class, this engine, because of its good boiler condition, was not scrapped but bought privately for preservation in 1968 and was donated by the owners to the North Eastern Locomotive Preservation Group in 1972. Since then the engine has undergone a major overhaul and restoration to resplendent L.N.E.R. Apple-Green livery as No. 2005. In 1974 2005 was delivered to the North Yorkshire Moors Railway where she can regularly be seen operating the passenger services.

M.B.

L.N.E.R. No. 3442 (K4) & No. 62005 (K1) at Staintondale A.M.B.

L.M.S. No. 43106 4 M.T. D. A. Idle

Exhibit No. 53.
Date 1951.
Railway Co.: L.M.S.
Loco Type: 2-6-0.
Loco Class: 4M.T.
Loco No.: 43106.
Normally exhibited to the public at Severn Valley Railway, Bridgnorth.

"Handsome is as handsome does" is clearly the motto with this design. This class was designed by H. G. Ivatt, the last Chief Mechanical Engineer of the L.M.S., and son of the famous H. A. Ivatt of the Great Northern Railway. Father's and son's locomotives were rugged, but the son went much further along the road of ease and simplicity of maintenance, when he turned out this design in 1947. Not even a mini-skirt! The wheels are in full view, and there is also no covering below the smokebox, where the stark front end is reminiscent of some German designs. Originally, the appearance of the class was even more unusual, as double chimneys were fitted, but later research work produced a more efficient chimney of conventional appearance.

This particular example was well travelled, working in East Anglia and the Midlands, and moving to Carlisle in 1966, where it worked freight to Kirkby Stephen and into Scotland. After slight damage due to a derailment at Colne, Lancs., it was withdrawn in 1968 and made its way in steam to Bridgnorth. *A.P.*

No. 75029 "Green Knight"

G. Davis

Exhibit No. 54. Date 1954.
Railway Co.: B.R.
Loco Type: 4-6-0.
Loco Class: 4M.T.
Loco No.: 75029.
Loco Name: Green Knight.
Normally exhibited to the public at East Somerset Railway, Cranmore.

No. 75029 was one of 80 class 4M.T. 4-6-0s built to the design of R. A. Riddles as one of his "mixed traffic" standard designs for British Railways. A development of the L.M.R. Class 4 2-6-4 tank, the new design incorporated modern features which served to enhance the reputation for speed, reliability and general effectiveness of its predecessor. With an axle load of 17 ¼ tons, the 4M.T.s could run almost anywhere and therefore became a very useful form of motive power for the less demanding duties for which they were designed. No. 75029 was the first of the class to have an improved front end incorporating a double chimney, and this design modification further improved an already popular machine. The locomotive was built at Swindon in 1954 and remained at work until withdrawn in 1967.

Purchased by Mr. David Shepherd in 1967, she was moved to Longmoor Camp in Hampshire during April 1968 and named *The Green Knight* in November 1969. In May 1970 she moved, in company with *Black Prince* to Liss in Hampshire as part of the stock of the Longmoor Steam Railway. From there she moved to Eastleigh Diesel Depot in October 1971 until the depot at Cranmore was built, and finally steamed down to Cranmore from Eastleigh on 17 November, 1973. The ownership of the engine was transferred to Mrs. Avril Shepherd about this time.

G.D.

Peter Robinson

No. 63395 Class Q6. Hard Slog

Freight Locomotives

Exhibit No. 61.
Date 1918.
Railway Co. N.E.R.
Loco Type: 0-8-0.
Loco Class: T2
Loco No.: 2238
Normally exhibited to the public at North Yorkshire Moors Railway, Grosmont.

Sir Vincent Raven's Class T2 0-8-0s, of which 120 were built between 1913 and 1918, were one of the most successful classes of freight engine designed and built by the North Eastern Railway at their Darlington Works. With 20"x 26" cylinders and 4' 7¼" wheels, these very powerful locomotives were built for hauling trains of 1,500 tons at 25 m.p.h. Fitted with a superheated boiler and steam reversing gear, they became an immediate success and were very popular with drivers all over the North Eastern Region. The design of these engines has never altered, except that in the 1930s several T2s were given older pattern tenders from the famous N.E.R. three-cylinder Atlantics. No. 2238 received one of these. This engine became No. 63395 after Nationalisation and with dieselisation approaching many newer steam engines available, the end of this numerous class seemed near. However, because of the ruggedness and reliability of this design, No. 2238 became one of the last steam engines working in the North East, eventually being withdrawn in September 1967. In a matter of months the engine was sold for scrap but by a very determined effort of North Eastern Locomotive Preservation Group members who raised the purchase price of £2,300 in just 5 months, it was saved from the breakers yard. After the locomotive was purchased. Group members have overhauled and fitted vacuum brakes to the engine for working passenger trains on the North Yorkshire Moors Railway where the engine feels quite "at home" climbing the 1 in 49 gradients between Grosmont and Goathland. In 1974-75 the engine underwent further restoration and has now been returned to North Eastern Railway livery in time for this exhibition and carried the crest of the famous railway company which built her 57 years ago.

M.B.
N.E.L.P.G.

No. 63395

N.E.R. No. 2392 Class P.3 N.E.L.P.G.

Exhibit No. 62.
Date 1923.
Railway Co.: N.E.R.
Loco Type 0-6-0.
Loco Class: P.3
Loco No.: 2392
Normally exhibited to the public at North Yorkshire Moors Railway, Grosmont.

By the 1980s, many of the North Eastern Railway 0-6-0 mineral engines were of Stockton & Darlington Railway design, like No. 1275 now part of the National Railway Museum collection.

With the appointment of T. W. Worsdell as Locomotive Superintendent in 1885, followed by his brother Wilson in 1890, a new era commenced and by 1910 521 0-6-0 engines had been built to improved designs. The new engines had clean lines, but the greatest innovation was the fitting of large cabs with side windows; these were so popular that they became a standard design for all N.E.R. tender locomotives.

The final development of these 0-6-0s was the Class P3, introduced in 1906 having a 5ft. 6ins. diameter boiler. No. 2392 was the last engine to be built in 1923, the year in which the North Eastern Railway amalgamated with other companies to form the L. & N.E.R. These largest of the N.E.R. 0-6-0s were powerful hard working engines which like the T2 0-8-0s lasted until the end of steam in the North East of England.

As J27 No. 65894, the engine was withdrawn from traffic in 1967 and was destined for the breakers yard. Fortunately the North Eastern Locomotion Preservation Group was formed in time for this example of a once-numerous class to be saved. Now fully overhauled and restored to N.E.R. livery as No. 2392, this engine is now enjoying a working retirement in the picturesque North Yorkshire Moors Railway.

M.B.

L.M.S. No. 8233 Class 8F

D. A. Idle

Exhibit No. 63.
Date 1935.
Railway Co.: L.M.S.
Loco Type: 2-8-0.
Loco Class: 8F.
Loco No. 8233.
Normally exhibited to the public at Severn Valley Railway, Bridgnorth.

There were altogether over 850 of these powerful locomotives built, by the L.M.S., other railway companies, and private builders. Many of them were very well travelled, a form of record in itself, as this standard heavy freight locomotive of the L.M.S. was adopted in 1940 as the wartime locomotive for the War Department, and the later "Austerity" engine was, more or less, an 8F redesigned for simplicity and more readily available materials.

Although built to a wartime order, No. 8233 served the L.M.S. for a year, until requisition in 1941. In the tradition of her class, she was well travelled, working in the Suez Canal Zone and Iran before returning to the Longmoor Military Railway in 1952. She was "demobbed" in 1957 as B.R. No. 48773, subsequently operating from Polmadie Shed, Glasgow and then Carlisle, Buxton and Rose Grove, in the years when an 8F hauling a seemingly endless freight train symbolised the end of the steam era.

In 1966, No. 48773 was given a major overhaul at Crewe Works, and as she was in the best all-round condition of all the 8Fs, she was purchased for preservation, as the result of a last-minute attempt by the Stanier 8F Locomotive Society. Now restored to full working order as No. 8233, her home is the Severn Valley Railway, where she regularly hauls passenger trains.

A.P.

Exhibit No. 64. **Date 1943.**
Railway Co.: W.D. **Loco Type: 2-10-0.**
Loco Class: 9F. **Loco No.: A.D. 600.**
Loco Name: Gordon.
Normally exhibited to the public at Severn Valley Railway, Bridgnorth.

No. 600 was the second locomotive of its class to be built to meet urgent wartime needs for the Ministry of Supply and, together with the more numerous 2-8-0 variant, the class totalled over 900. Most of these locomotives were sent overseas towards the end of the second World War to assist in restoring rail traffic in many different countries. However, No. 600 remained in England for use by the British Army for instructional purposes at the Longmoor Military Railway in Hampshire.

After the cessation of hostilities, most of the "Austerity" locomotives were returned to the United Kingdom and were loaned to the British Railway companies to assist in freight haulage. Twenty five of the 2-10-0s, some seven hundred of the 2-8-0s and a number of 0-6-0 saddle tanks (represented by Exhibit 77); were subsequently taken into British Railways' stock and remained in service until the mid 1960s. Many other examples also survived in Europe and Scandinavia for many years after the war.

The production difficulties and material shortages associated with wartime were the criteria which compelled the designer to produce a locomotive which was flexible, powerful, yet easy to build and maintain. This was successfully achieved and it is noticeable that this locomotive does not carry any unnecessary embellishments and that the outline is stark and businesslike when compared with other exhibits.

To enable the locomotive to use lightly laid tracks with curves as sharp as 4½ chains radius, the centre driving wheel is flangeless, while the second and fourth drivers have narrow flanges. The axle loading of this locomotive is only 12½ tons and this, together with its flexibility, enabled it to reach destinations that had not previously been accessible to large locomotives.

No. 600 was named *Gordon* after the famous General Gordon, whilst its sister engine No. 601, since withdrawn from Longmoor, was named *Kitchener.*

The locomotive is shown in the final livery used by the British Army for its steam locomotives, having carried previous liveries of khaki and green.

K.A.L.

600 "Gordon" D. A. Idle

B.R. No. 92220 "Evening Star" 9.F. I. G. Holt

Exhibit No. 66.
Date 1960.
Railway Co.: British Rail.
Loco Type: 2-10-0.
Loco Class: 9F.
Loco No.: 92220.
Loco Name: Evening Star.
Normally exhibited to the public at the National Railway Museum, York.

When the last steam locomotive was constructed for British Railways in 1960, the name chosen was *Evening Star,* thus recalling an earlier engine of that name, built by Robert Stephenson & Co. for the Great Western Railway in 1839. But, whereas the original *Evening Star* had only 2 driving wheels, the last had 10. Swindon made a great day out of her naming, and the locomotive was finished in lined Brunswick green, instead of the sombre black of her sisters.

Her lines were impressive, but functional; gone are the days when "the works" were tucked out of sight for the sake of appearance, to the despair of the maintenance staff. This is functional and efficient design. With more wheels—and power—than most, the 9Fs did a big job all over the country on heavy freights. In this area they could be seen hauling huge iron-ore trains up the heavy gradients to Consett Iron Works. They also appeared on passenger trains; fast passenger trains, which got faster, until a maximum of 90 m.p.h. was reported! This came to the ears of Someone in Authority, who worked out how fast those small wheels would be turning, and what would happen if that huge coupling rod flew off! Authority (regretfully, one hopes) said desist! But the 9F had made its name as a very efficient machine indeed. With its reputation, its functionally attractive lines (when not equipped, as some were, with patent boilers and chimneys in the name of economy), the last of Britain's steam locomotives was a worthy conclusion to a fine tradition.

A.P.

Shunting Locomotives

Exhibit No. 71.
Date 1857.
Railway Co.: Wantage Tramway.
Loco Type: 0-4-0 WT.
Loco No.: 5.
Loco Name: Shannon.
Normally exhibited to the public at Great Western Society, Didcot.

This engine, now restored to full working condition, is probably the oldest engine capable of being steamed in the British Isles. She was originally built for a private line, the Sandy and Potton Railway and carried the name of *Shannon.* From there she came into the hands of the London & North Western Railway who used her as their working shunter at Crewe before selling her in 1878 for £365 8s. 1d. She became No. 5 on the Wantage Tramway and unofficially was known as *Jane.* The Wantage Tramway was one of the first roadside tramways in this country to be authorised to use steam. Steam-powered country tramways were never common in this country though they were on the Continent. The Wantage Tramway ran for just under 3 miles from the Great Western main line at Wantage Road Station to the small Berkshire market town of Wantage. Passenger service ceased in 1925. However, there was sufficient work to keep *Jane* occupied until the line closed in 1945. The Great Western Railway bought her for £100 in April, 1946, at the clearance sale, restored her original name of *Shannon* and placed her on a plinth at Wantage Road Station. When this station closed she was removed to Didcot and overhauled. Since that time she has been in steam on several occasions.

M.W.

H. C. Casserley

Left: *No. 5 Near Wantage*
Below: *Wantage Tramway No. 5 "Shannon" in Tramway days.*

British Rail

Exhibit No. 73.
Date 1891.
Railway Co.: N.E.R.
Loco Type: 0-4-0T.
Loco Class: H1.
Loco No.: 1310.
Normally exhibited to the public at Middleton Railway, Hunslet, Leeds.

The clean lines of this locomotive are typical of the style of several classes built for the North Eastern Railway at the end of the last century. These smart little engines worked goods yards and docks throughout the North East. The London & North Eastern Railway built more of them in 1923 (Class Y7). However, many were retired into colliery service in the 1930s. One of these engines had its "hour of glory" working the passenger service on the privately-owned North Sunderland Railway from Chathill to Seahouses in Northumberland.

The Trustees acquired 1310 from the N.C.B. in 1965, when it was about to be scrapped at Watergate Colliery. It has been carefully restored by the Trustees and is presented in the North Eastern Railway green livery. This locomotive can be seen working on Steam open days at the Middleton Railway, Leeds.

It is particularly interesting to compare the style of this locomotive with that of the D.S.B. 385 exhibit No. 72. A.B.

W. Hampson

N.E.R. Class H 1310

D.S.B. 385 Class HSII W. Hampson

Exhibit No. 72.
Date 1895.
Railway Co.: Danish State Railway.
Loco Type: 0-4-0WT.
Loco Class: HSII.
Loco No.: 385.
Normally exhibited to the public at Middleton Railway, Hunslet, Leeds.

A typical continental engine which appears to have all and sundry attached to the outside. This engine was built by Hartmann in Germany. However, Neilsons of Glasgow also constructed locomotives of this design for Denmark. They were used to shunt wagons in goods depots and factories. On the docks they moved wagons and coaches on and off the car ferries between Jylland, Fyn, and Sjaelland. Its chimney rivals that of *Locomotion* for height. The locomotive is "out of gauge" for British Railways so it cannot take part in the cavalcade. Like all Danish State Railway locomotives the national colours are carried as a band round the base of the chimney. This engine is fitted with electric lights and has both a bell and a whistle. At the time it was purchased by Steam Power Trust 65 it was at Odense, and was transported from there low loader to the Middleton Railway at Leeds in September, 1972.

A.B.

Exhibit No. 74.
Date 1901.
Railway Co.: G.W.R.
Loco Type: 0-6-0 ST.
Loco No.: 813.
Normally exhibited to the public at the Severn Valley Railway, Bridgnorth.

No. 813 was originally built by Hudswell Clarke & Co. of Leeds as one of six identical saddle tanks for the Port Talbot Railway, a small company which operated the docks at Port Talbot and several short branch lines into the nearby coalfields. As P.T.R. No. 26 it was absorbed into G.W.R. stock in 1908 when the Port Talbot system was taken over by the G.W.R. It did not, however, receive its G.W.R. number (813) until the grouping of 1923.

Meanwhile, the locomotive was maintained at Swindon and gradually acquired its present 'hybrid' nature. This is, perhaps, best typified by its standard G.W.R. coal bunker and unmistakable brass safety valve bonnet mounted somewhat incongruously on the dome cover.

In the 1930s the locomotive was offered for sale and its was thus that No. 813 found itself in unfamiliar surroundings as a pit shunter at Backworth Colliery, Northumberland early in 1934.

As Backworth No. 12 (later N.C.B. No. 11) she remained exiled in the north for over thirty years until the mounting pace of pit closures and the associated availability of more modern locomotive types rendered her redundant for the second time in 1967. It was at this point that the current owners purchased the locomotive for permanent preservation. It was later moved to Bridgnorth on the Severn Valley Railway where the lengthy task of restoration to 1930 running condition and G.W.R. livery was subsequently commenced.

W.H.

G.W.R. No. 813

J. Ray

No. 51218 "Pug" at Haworth I. G. Holt

Exhibit No. 75.
Date 1901.
Railway Co.: Lancashire & Yorkshire Railway.
Loco Type: 0-4-0 ST.
Loco Class: "Pug".
Loco No.: 51218.
Normally exhibited to the public at Keighley & Worth Valley Railway.

Fifty seven "Pugs", diminutive 0-4-0 saddle tanks for use in sharply curved sidings, were built by the Lancashire & Yorkshire Railway between 1891 and 1910. They were allocated for service in the industrial and dockland areas of Goole, Fleetwood, Liverpool and Salford. Later, in L.M.S. days, they became more widely dispersed, reaching such places as Bristol, Bangor, Crewe, Derby, Widnes, York and Swansea.

Two of these engines survive today. No. 51218 was the first locomotive to arrive at Haworth (in January 1964) under the auspices of the Society and after overhaul was one of the first to be steamed, quickly becoming a favourite with drivers and visitors alike. It has spent some 2½ years away from Haworth since, working enthusiasts' excursions in Rochdale and Manchester, returning in November 1969. It was also loaned for two periods to Messrs. Brown & Polson at Trafford Park whilst their own loco was under repair.

K.W.V.R.

Exhibit No. 77
Date 1943.
Railway Co.: N.C.B.
Class: L.N.E.R./ J.94. 0-6-0 ST. (Type).
In service with N.C.B.

During the war it became apparent that there was a need for a powerful shunting locomotive for use at home and abroad. This locomotive was designed by the Hunslet Engine Co., at Leeds and manufactured by the leading locomotive companies for the Ministry of Supply.

After the war they were acquired by the L.N.E.R. and production continued for use by private companies. Many of these locomotives are still in service in works and collieries.

A.B.

L.N.E.R. No. 54 Sentinel W. Hampson

Coal Train K. Lummas

Exhibit No. 76.
Date 1933.
Railway Co.: L.N.E.R.
Loco Type: 0-4-0 Sentinel.
Loco Class: Y1.
Loco No.: 54.
Normally displayed to the public at Middleton Railway, Hunslet, Leeds.

This is a typical Sentinel locomotive fitted with a 275 lb/sq. in. water tubed vertical boiler. An adaption of their steam road vehicles, it has the cylinders mounted vertically and the drive is then transmitted to the wheels by chains, this being in marked contrast to standard railway practice. These engines are light, easy to handle and could raise steam quite quickly, making them eminently suitable for moving wagons, in goods depots and workshops. This locomotive spent most of its life at Darlington working in the Geneva Road Reclamation Depot. In June 1961 it was acquired by the Middleton Railway and operates at Leeds.

A.M.B.

Diesel & Petrol Locomotives

Exhibit No. 81.
Date 1918.
Railway Co.: Industrial.
Loco Type: Petrol 4W. Simplex.
Loco No.: 1364.
Normally exhibited to the public at North of England Open Air Museum, Beamish.

This is an interesting survival of the first World War, as this type of armour plated locomotive was used by the Railway Operating Division of the Royal Engineers to bring up ammunition to the front line trenches. As they gave off no smoke or steam they were practically invisible. Several examples of this type of engine, which had a robust construction and was very reliable, survived until comparatively recent years—a much longer life than had originally been planned. This example still has its original 4 cylinder 40 h.p. Dorman engine. Originally this was a 60 cm (2 feet) gauge engine but it has been regauged to standard 4′ 8½″ and fitted with normal height buffing gear. After War Department use this engine went to Newalls works at Sandyford near Paisley in Scotland and from there to their factory at Washington, County Durham. A narrow gauge Simplex of similar vintage can be seen on the Festiniog Railway in North Wales.

M.W.

Armoured Locomotive M. Wheeler

Exhibit No. 82.
Date 1916.
Railway Co.: Industrial.
Loco Type: Petrol 4W.
Loco Class: 60 h.p.
Loco No. 680.
Loco Name: Jacob.
Normally exhibited to the public at Dinting Steam Centre.

This example of an early petrol industrial engine is very interesting and is one of the oldest working internal-combustion locomotives surviving. Baguleys in 1916 were building petrol locomotives that were in advance of any others at the time. These engines were designed to compete with steam engines but not as a cheap substitute. Hence they were expensive to buy but long lasting. They could cope with up to 90 tons on the level. This engine was originally delivered to Richard Johnson and Nephew Limited at their Munitions works at Aintree, Liverpool and passed from them to Jacob's Biscuit Factory also at Aintree. A new Baguley 60 h.p. engine replaced the original White and Poppe in 1927. In 1968 it was overhauled and repainted and presented by Jacob's Biscuits to the Open Air Museum. The large cylindrical tank contains cooling liquid.

M.W.

Exhibit No. 83.
Date 1933.
Railway Co.: L.M.S./W.D.
Loco Type: 0-4-0 D.
Loco No.: 7050/240.
On active service.

This was the early diesel shunting locomotive tried by the L.M.S. No. 7050 was a two-axle unit designed by the Drewry Car Co. Ltd., and built at the English Electric Company's Preston works.

680 at Jacob's Biscuit Factory M. Wheeler

Carrying Drewry works No. 2047, it was put into service in 1934 and had a 176 h.p. W. K. Allen 8RS18 eight-cylinder in-line engine, and the now familiar Vulcan-Sinclair fluid coupling. It included also a Wilson four-speed epi-cyclic gearbox with jackshaft and side-rod final drive by Bostock & Bramley. The speed range was 2.9, 5.1, 8.5 and 12 m.p.h. Weight in working order was 26 tons, wheelbase 7 ft., wheel diameter 36 in., maximum tractive effort 11,200 lb., top speed 12 m.p.h.

Before delivery, it was put on trial in Preston Docks early in May 1934 and found capable of handling trains of 400 tons weight. After operating mainly in Salford Goods Yard, it was sent on loaon in 1940 to the War Department and eventually purchased by them in March 1943. It is believed still in operation with the W.D., although now with a 153 h.p. Gardner 6L3 six-cylinder engine and a new Wilson-Drewry air-operated gearbox.

B.W.

L.M.S. No. 7050 at Preston B. Webb

Coaches and Rolling Stock

Passenger Coaches & Wagons
It is the powerful express locomotives that tend to dominate any railway exhibition. However, there are some enthusiasts who devote their skill and care to the restoration of coaches. I feel sure that visitors will appreciate the coaches displayed.

FLYING SCOTSMAN ENTERPRISES
Several coaches have been fitted out to provide accommodation and administrative facilities for the support crew for *Flying Scotsman.* Of particular interest are:

101 G.E.R. No. 1 General Manager's Inspection Saloon.

102 L.N.E.R. No. 24287 Restaurant Buffet Gresley 1939.

103 G.W.R. No. 9004 Officer's Saloon.

GREAT WESTERN SOCIETY—DIDCOT
The Great Western Society present a finely restored train which is used for their special excursions. The picture shows the quality of the work done on the upholstery.

111 G.W.R. Open Third Excursion Coach 1289/1938.

112 G.W.R. Compartment Third Corridor 536/1940.

113 G.W.R. Compartment Composite Corridor 7313/1940.

114 G.W.R. Brake Composite Corridor 7371/1941.

115 G.W.R. Special Saloon Car 9002/1940.

116 G.W.R. Siphon G. 2796/1937.

6000 LOCOMOTIVE ASSOCIATION

121 Pullman Coach "Aquila."

122 Composite Corridor.

NORTH EASTERN RAILWAY COACH GROUP
This group are restoring a N.E.R. Auto Coach which was an attempt to operate conveniently and economically country

Director's Coach G.E.R. No. 1

Bousfield

First Class Restoration F. Dumbleton

branch lines. The coach on completion will be displayed on the North Yorkshire Moors Railway.

125 N.E.R.—Clerestory Auto Coach No. 3453/190A.

127 POST OFFICE T.P.O.

A travelling post office used for sorting mail will be displayed in association with the Post Office presentation.

RAILWAY PRESERVATION SOCIETY

This group have their headquarters at Chasewater Park, Brownhills, Staffs. The Maryport & Carlisle Coach finished its active life as part of the miner's paddy train at a nearby colliery. Illustrated is another coach in a similar condition to the Maryport & Carlisle coach when its was recovered.

131 Six wheel Maryport & Carlisle Coach 1875.

SCOTTISH & NEWCASTLE BREWERIES LTD.

Excellent meals were to be had on such trains as the Tyne Tees Pullman, Brighton Belle, Queen of Scots etc. Many Pullman coaches have been adapted to extend the restaurant facilities of small inns and hotels.

135 Pullman Coach 301.

136 Pullman Coach 308.

N.E.R. Auto Train

SCOTTISH RAILWAY PRESERVATION SOCIETY

At their depot in Falkirk the society have restored several coaches for use on their special excursions and on the branch line when it opens.

141 Caledonian Railway Composite Corridor Brake, St. Rollox/1921.

142 North British Invalid Saloon, Cowlairs /1919.

TYSELEY STEAM CENTRE

From the collection on display at Tyseley Steam Centre the following coach is presented:—

145 G.W.R. Officers Saloon 80972.

STRATHSPEY RAILWAY

The company are preparing stock to re-open the line from Aviemore to Boat of Garten, Inverness. Clearly a magnificent job has been made of these coaches and they will be a pleasure to ride in.

Restoration begins here—M.S.L.R. Coach

B. Ball

B.R. Sleeping Car 394 — W. E. C. Watkinson

The Highland Railway Van was built in July, 1876. However, after 30 years working life it was used as temporary sleeping quarters for the signalmen at the remote Inchlea signal box. No doubt it was also a welcome refuge for platelayers as well in stormy weather.

151 Highland Railway 4 wheel luggage van No. 5/1876.

152 L.M.S. 6 wheel luggage van No. 33003 Wolverton/1939.

153 L.M.S. Tourist Open Coach No. 77234 Wolverton/1945.

154 B.R. 12 wheeled First class sleeping car 394 Wolverton/1951.

VINTAGE CARRIAGE TRUST

The Trust are restoring several coaches on the Keighley & Worth Valley Railway. The restored coach from the Manchester, Sheffield & Lincolnshire Railway should be compared to the dilapidated coach illustrated on the adjacent page.

161 M.S.L.R. Six Wheel Compartment Coach 176/1876.

162 N.E.R. Inspection Saloon 1661/1871.

163 S.R. Corridor Brake Third 3854/1924.

Bluebell Railway

170 L.B.S.C.R. Wagon 3346.

EAST SOMERSET RAILWAY

175 S.R. S1000S Prototype Fibreglass Coach.

Highland Railway Luggage Van No. 5

Commuter Trains

Exhibit No. 91.
Date 1922.
Railway Co.: Metropolitan Railway.
.Loco Type: Electric Bo-Bo.
Loco No.: 12.
Loco Name: Sarah Siddons.
In Departmental Service.

This locomotive was one of twenty Bo-Bo 1200 h.p. electric locomotives built for the Metropolitan Railway by Vickers Ltd. of Barrow-in-Furness in 1922/23. All were withdrawn from passenger service by 1961 following completion of the Metropolitan Line modernisation scheme and the transfer of the Aylesbury service to British Railways. Four were retained for the time being by London Transport for shunting and miscellaneous duties and No. 12 is now the only one remaining in use—as an engineering test vehicle while No. 5 is preserved in the London Transport collection at Syon Park.

The 20 locomotives were built principally to haul the longer-distance Metropolitan trains of compartment coaches between the City, Baker Street and the Aylesbury Line—at this time as far as Harrow-on-the-Hill; a steam locomotive took over for the rest of the journey. With the extension of electrification to Rickmansworth in 1925, the locomotive changeover point was moved there. The electric locomotives were also used to haul a number of through trains of the G.W.R. between Paddington and the City until the outbreak of the last war, and on local freight trains.

Metropolitan Electric No. 12 Sarah Siddons L.T.E.

Exhibit No. 92.
Date 1971.
Railway Co.: London Transport Exec.
Electric Multiple Unit, 3 Car Unit.
In Service.

The example displayed is a 3 car unit from one of the 88 trains on Piccadilly line to be completely replaced during the summer of 1975.

The external finish is of unpainted aluminium except for a deep red band across the lower section of the cab front. The double length, double glazed side windows of the Victoria Line Stock are adopted for the new trains also as are the higher windows in the doors which enable a passenger standing in the vestibule to see his station name without stooping.

Inside, the appearance is very similar to that of the Victoria Line train with moquette covered seats, extensive use of plastic finishes, fluorescent lighting and illuminated advertisements. Glass screens at the doors are set farther back from the door opening. This "stand back" space being specially provided to accommodate luggage without obstructing the doors. Each car has 44 seats arranged in longitudinal and transverse formation similar to that of the existing Piccadilly Line train.

With the possibility of eventual automatic train operation in mind on a line with long open air sections it is considered that some form of new braking system with slip/slide protection is needed for individual cars. To achieve individual car protection the "Westcote" electro numatic braking system in an "energise to release" form is used for the new stock. This system allows individual car-load control to be used instead of the retardation control previously used. Loss of the electrical feed to the system causes the cars brakes to be applied. The circuitry is so arranged that emergencies requiring automatic brake application, such as the operation of the alarm by a passenger, the train being "tripped" at a signal at "danger" etc., can all be dealt with by the new system.

To help the driver a new fault annunciator system is being developed to indicate in the cab either actual faults which have imobilised the train or potential faults which could lead to immobilisation.

This should mean that delays caused by defective trains can be greatly reduced.

Piccadilly Line 3 Car Unit L.T.E.

Prototype Train for Tyne-Wear Metro Metro Cammell

Exhibit No. 93.
Date 1974.
Railway Co.: Tyne/Wear Metro.
Mock up of prototype car.

From this wooden mock-up, built by Metro-Cammell Limited, the design for the prototype cars which are now undergoing tests in the Newcastle area was jointly developed by the Tyne and Wear Passenger Transport Executive and Metro-Cammell Limited.

The cars are designed to provide passenger services both on the surface and underground, and have fabricated steel bogies, steel body framing, aluminium body panels and roof sheets, and moulded glass-reinforced plastic driving ends which are designed and constructed to confine any possible collision damage to local areas.

The cars are capable of being driven from either end and can be operated singly or in trains of up to 3 cars. They are designed for one-man operation and are fitted with automatic couplers.

Current collection is via a single pantograph from an overhead supply of 1500 volts D.C.

In the selection of equipments to be used, special consideration has been given to reducing the operating noise to a minimum by the adoption of such features as hypoid gears and resilient wheels.

Each car has two powered bogies one at each outer end, and a nonpowered bogie under the centre articulation. The powered bogies incorporate a single motor with two output shafts.

Heating and ventilation is provided by waste heat from the resistors, which by use of linked dampers, operated by remote control, can supply warm air to the car in cold weather and in warm weather can ventilate the car by extracting air.

Statistics

Seating capacity	84
Standing capacity at 6 per/m²	188
Maximum speed	80 km/h

Puffing Billy outside George Stephenson's House. This locomotive is displayed to the public in the Science Museum, London. Frank Graham Newcastle. Painter—Embleton

RECOMMENDED READING:

Stockton & Darlington Railway

1. History of the Stockton & Darlington Railway. *Jeans 1875, Longman Reprint 1974. Frank Graham, Newcastle.*
2. Stockton & Darlington Railway, Previous Celebrations. *Hoole 1974, Dalesman*
3. Stockton & Darlington Railway—A Pictorial Survey. *Hoole 1975, David & Charles.*
4. Exploring the Stockton & Darlington Railway, *Semmens 1975, Frank Graham, Newcastle.*
5. Stockton & Darlington Railway—150 Years of British Railways, *Adams, Semmens, Whitehouse, 1975 New English Library.*
6. Rail 150: The Stockton & Darlington Railway and What Followed, *Semmens 1975, Eyre Methuen.*
7. History of the North Eastern Railway, *Tomlinson 1914, Longman, Reprint David & Charles 1972.*
8. Northern Echo. Stockton & Darlington Railway Centenary Edition 1925, *Reprint 1975.*
9. The Stockton & Darlington Railway and the New Town of Middlesbrough. Circa 200 pages, of extracts from Official Documents, Private papers, and contemporary Newspapers. Specially prepared for Schools and Students and available from Cleveland County Council, Schools Museum Service, Halifax Buildings, Exchange Place, Middlesbrough. (Summer 1975).
10. Stockton & Darlington Railway. Resources Kit for Junior & Secondary Schools. Facsimile Documents, Maps, Biographies. Guide to S. & D. Railway, Colour pictures etc. 1975. *Frank Graham, 6 Queens Tce., Jesmond, Newcastle-upon-Tyne.*

Railway Preservation

Steam 75. *Handbook of Association of Railway Preservation Societies. Annually Haratton Press.*

Preserved Locomotives Vol. 1a British Isles, Vol. 1b Europe, Vol. II Americas, Vol. III *Wildish, Railway Preservation Society, 42 Frensham Road, Southsea.*

Preserved Locomotives,*Casserley 1973, Ian Allen, Third Edition.*

The New Image

The Victorians who pioneered the age of rail, steam and speed thrust transport into the 20th Century. Now **British Rail** is developing trends that will show the way into the 21st Century.

Inter-City, Railfreight, Motorail, Golden Rail, British Rail Engineering Ltd., Seaspeed, Sealink—they all contribute to British Rail's new image. It's an image that combines vastly different activities.

Take Seaspeed, who were first to operate giant, car-carrying hovercraft across the Channel commercially. They bring Boulogne and Calais within thirty-five minutes of Britain.

Sealink's passenger, car and commercial vehicle ferries sail ten routes between Britain and Europe and operate services between Britain, Ireland and the Channel Islands. British Rail's latest ship, the 9,000 ton *St Edmund,* is the largest in the Sealink fleet, which is operated jointly with continental partners.

Golden Rail, with its 46 holiday resorts, takes British Rail into the home package holiday field, and the network of Motorail trains opens a new dimension for many thousands of Britain's motorists who like to travel with their families in comfort, while the car travels behind on the same train.

Seaspeed Hovercraft

Rail Freight

The 13 main works of British Rail Engineering Ltd. make the railways' manufacturing giant one of the largest engineering concerns in the country. The company builds and maintains British Rail's locomotives, wagons and coaches, and builds equipment and rolling stock for outside industry, taking its place among the world's leading rolling stock manufacturers. Shildon, the largest wagon works, repairs up to 800 wagons a week and is building over 1,000 high-capacity coal wagons and freight vans for British Rail.

But at the hub of British Rail are the diesel and electrically-hauled trains of Inter-City and Railfreight.

Inter-City stands for 1,800 expresses that run daily over 6,000 route miles, linking 200 principal cities and towns.

It's a highly developed business and one that is constantly being improved. There's nothing unusual now about 100 m.p.h. trains, and Inter-City's modern, air-conditioned coaches set a standard of luxury that ranks with Europe's foremost expresses.

At night Inter-City runs 70 sleeper trains serving 100 destinations in business and holiday areas—that's nearly 7,000 beds on the move every night.

Today's Inter-City showpiece is the electrified West Coast main line, where the fastest trains eat up 401 miles between London and Glasgow in five hours.

Tomorrow it will be the turn of the London-Bristol and South Wales routes, where a new era in rail travel is already being ushered in by the 125 m.p.h. High Speed Train (H.S.T.). More journey times will be cut when H.S.T.s take over services on the East Coast main line between London and Edinburgh and other principal routes.

Still further ahead it will be the turn of the Advanced Passenger Train (A.P.T.), now being developed at British Rail's technical centre at Derby and capable of running at 150 m.p.h. on existing track. The A.P.T. is an energy-efficient, high-performance train which exploits improved guidance techniques and body tilt to negotiate curves at high speed.

But Inter-City is only part of the story. Equally important to industrial customers is Railfreight, which daily demonstrates its specialist role in moving bulk loads swiftly over long distances.

Coal, steel, oil, roadstone, cement and new motorcars are some of the commodities that move about the country in entire trainloads, accounting for three quarters of the 180 million tons that go Railfreight each year.

High Speed Train

Advanced Passenger Train

A giant oil train of 2,000 tons running between private sidings at refinery and power station relieves the roads of around 100 oil tankers. Industry is cashing in on this built-in advantage of rail transport by using more private sidings every year, and investing millions in fleets of privately-owned wagons to carry specific materials.

But a modern railway needs more than electric and diesel locomotives and new rolling stock. By the side of the track more and more multi-aspect colour-light signals are appearing, replacing the traditional semaphores.

They represent a switch from mechanical to electrical signalling, which enables one power signal centre to control a hundred or more miles of track, taking over the work of dozens of old-fashioned manual signalboxes.

There can be no doubt about rail's ability to adapt. In the last 20 years this has been proved beyond doubt, as the transport scene has become more intense and competitive.

Modern developments and techniques are opening up still further potential and, given the investment, British Rail will be playing a vital role in British transport when the 200th Anniversary of railways come in AD2025. **B.R.** ©

Grand Steam Cavalcade K. Hoole

The climax of the week of celebrations marking the 150th Anniversary of the Stockton & Darlington Railway, running from 24-31 August, will take the form of a Grand Steam Cavalcade, which will start from the Rail 150 Exhibition at Shildon's British Rail Engineering Workshops along the line of the original track to Heighinton where *Locomotion* was first put on the rails. It is anticipated that over thirty steam locomotives will take part, including such famous names as *Flying Scotsman, Leander* and *Sir Nigel Gresley.* They will pass the grandstands and viewing points along the track for a period of over two hours, commencing at 14.00 hrs. on Sunday 31st August. The order of their procession is not yet finalised. However a copy of the supplementary sheet will be available free on the presentation of this guide.

In 1925 the Centenary Celebrations took the form of a procession of fifty-three old and new locomotives from Stockton to Fighting Cocks, along the course of the original Stockton & Darlington line, followed by an extensive display of locomotives, coaches, and old and new railway items, in Faverdale Wagon Works, which had been built a few years previously. The engines in the Procession ranged from *Locomotion,* which hauled the first train in 1825, to the new Gresley Pacific *William Whitelaw,* named in honour of the Chairman of the L.N.E.R. This was a class of engine which performed such excellent work on the East Coast main line between London, York, Newcastle, and Edinburgh. *Locomotion,* which was the last exhibit in the Procession, was actually propelled by a petrol engine hidden in the tender, and it was preceded by a man on horseback, carrying a red flag, to give warning of the train's approach. Behind *Locomotion* came a string of chaldron wagons—an early form of coal wagon—and a replica of the coach used by the Directors of the company. This was, however, little more than a large box on wheels, with openings cut in the sides for windows, and at the ends for doors. It had no springs and the passengers sat facing one another on wooden seats stretching down each side. The chaldron wagons were filled with passengers in period costume, and included a band.

After the Procession and the Faverdale Exhibition *Locomotion* was returned to its plinth at Bank Top station, Darlington, where it had stood since 1892. It had previously been on display in the open air at North Road station from 1857.

Photomatic

S. & D. Railway No. 1275.
1925 Celebration Procession

John Wigston

Locomotive No. 1

National Railway Museum

Material from many museums has been collected together by the Department of Education & Science.

The National Railway Museum, which will be opened by His Royal Highness The Duke of Edinburgh on 27th September, 1975, illustrates the history and development of British railway engineering including the social and economic aspects.

The collection contains some 25 loco- from the *Agenoria* of 1829 including *Mallard* and a fully sectioned rebuilt Merchant Navy Class 4-6-2; 22 items of rolling stock, as well as signalling equipment and permanent way items. Small exhibits will feature models of locomotives (many of them working) and rolling stock; also a wide variety of railway equipment and material, including uniforms, station furniture, name plates, bridge models and other categories of relics associated with the past 150 years of railways in the United Kingdom. There will also be displays and reference collections of paintings, posters, photographs, drawings and films. A reference library service will be provided by appointment.

A Lecture Theatre seating 70 is incorporated in the building and a programme of lecture-demonstrations will be established together with routine and on-request guided tours. A shop is being provided which will stock railway books, postcards, slides etc.

The Museum will be open from 10 a.m. until 6 p.m. on weekdays and from 2.30 p.m. until 6 p.m. on Sundays. The Museum is closed on Christmas Eve, Christmas Day, Boxing Day, New Year's Day and Good Friday. Admission will be free.

The Museum is within a few minutes walk of York railway station. Car parking is available at the Museum.

National Railway Museum P. W. B. Semmens

Rail Trail

Alan Batty

Locomotion Trust

Visitors to the exhibition of steam locomotives may also wish to take the opportunity of seeing many things of railway and industrial archaeological interest in the immediate area, some of which have been specially arranged to form part of the celebrations. Foremost amongst these is the "Rail Trail" extending westwards from Shildon to the original starting point of the Stockton & Darlington railway at Witton Park. This trail will be primarily a foot trail and it will be possible to traverse long sections of the original rail bed. The Rail Trail Guide shows clearly the sections of the trail to which the public have access and visitors are strongly recommended to obtain a copy before setting out on the trail.

In conjunction with the rail trail an audio visual centre will be operating at Shildon where a commentary, illustrated by slides, will describe some of the history of the railway and features along the route.

In contrast to this western portion of the line, the section from Stockton to Shildon is either occupied by the present B.R. track or has been built over. This means that it is not possible to walk over a track bed between the various points of interest, and as these are some distance apart and public roads have to be used, this section is most conveniently traversed by car.

Leaflets identifying the places of interest will be on sale at the old S. & D. booking office at St. John's Crossing in Stockton, and at Preston Park Museum, through which passes a section of the original Stockton & Darlington railway embankment.

TIMOTHY HACKWORTH'S HOUSE, SHILDON, CO. DURHAM.

IDEAS FOR A DAY OUT

Throughout the north east are collections of railway and technical items on display to the public which are fascinating to all the family and make a good reason for a day out.

1. DARLINGTON

a **Darlington Museum, Tubwell Row:** Open Mon to Fri, 10.00 to 13.00, 14.00 to 18.00. Thurs 10.00 to 13.00. Sat 10.00 to 13.00, 14.00 to 17.30.
Contains a fine presentation on the Stockton & Darlington Railway and George Stephenson.

b **North Road Station Museum, Darlington:** Open (To be announced).
To be the home of *Locomotion* and *Derwent.*

c **Darlington Station,** Bank Top (Open continuously).
At present *Locomotion* and *Derwent* are on a plinth at the station.

2a

2. STOCKTON-ON-TEES

a **Stockton & Darlington Railway Booking Office:** Open Mon to Sat, 10.00 to 18.00.
Set up as a museum containing much interesting material.

b **Preston Hall Museum:** Open Mon to Sat 10.00 to 18.00. Sun 14.00 to 18.00.
An interesting exhibition of material associated with the Stockton & Darlington Railway and the town.
Yarm High Street & Viaduct.

3. BEAMISH, Co. Durham—(Chester-le-Street to Stanley).

a **North of England Open Air Museum.** Open Easter to October, Tues to Sun and Bank Holidays 10.00 to 18.00, last entry 17.00. Closed Mondays.
The collection contains the Hetton Colliery Locomotive (1823) and many other items of railway interest.

b **Marley Hill Steam Centre:** Open occasional week-ends.
A group of enthusiasts have established a collection of industrial locomotives from the North East.

3a

4. SUNDERLAND

a **Monkwearmouth Station Museum:** Open Mon to Fri 09.30 to 17.30. Sat 09.30 to 16.00.
An impress station facade, finely restored, housing an interesting collection of local items including railway photographs.

b **Bridges:** Note also the bridges over the River Wear.

5. NEWCASTLE-UPON-TYNE

a **Museum of Science & Engineering:** Open Mon, Wed, Fri, Sat 10.00 to 18.00. Tues, Thurs 10.00 to 20.00. Sun 14.30 to 17.30.
Exhibition Park. A fascinating collection of transport relics including Stephenson's Killingworth engine "Billy".

b **Bridges:** Newcastle central station & the Tyne Bridges are worthy of mention.

4a

6. NORTH YORKSHIRE MOORS RAILWAY Grosmont—Goathland—Pickering.
Signed from the Middlesbrough to Whitby road. Open daily in summer.
The opportunity of a delightful train journey through Newtondale, together with an interesting collection of restored working steam locomotives.

5a

7. SHILDON, Hackworth Museum. Wed. to Sun. 10.00 to 17.00.

8. GEORGE STEPHENSON'S BIRTH-PLACE, Wylam on Tyne. External viewing only.

9. GEORGE STEPHENSON'S HOUSE, Killingworth. External viewing only.

10. NATIONAL RAILWAY MUSEUM, YORK. (After 27th September, 1975)

NORTHUMBRIA TOURIST BOARD

A leaflet giving further information about places of interest and accommodiation is available from the Board's offices, Prudential Buildings, 140/150 Pilgrim Street, Newcastle-upon-Tyne.